# Laugh Now, Cry Later

## Graham McClements

Dedicated to: Sandra, Arlene, Gordon, Alison, Audrey and Maxwell – who did their best to keep me humble!

*Some of the names and places have been changed to protect the innocent!*

# Contents

# Foreword

When Graham asked me to say a few words in a foreword for this book I was very apprehensive, having known some of the antics he got up to. But after a few minutes I realised it would be a book full of many interesting insights.

I first met Graham in 1973 when I was General Manager of the *Slieve Donard Hotel*. He was one of the chefs in the Kitchen Brigade and then showed signs of an eventful future. His talents as a chef were obvious as he was shoulders above all other young chefs. After my time in the *Slieve* I've always kept an eye on what he was at and believe me you will enjoy reading this book.

I am amazed at Graham's achievements over the years and wonder what part I will play in his memories. One thing comes to mind and it took place in July 1975. I will leave you all to read the book and find out for yourselves if he recalls the incident.

Enjoy the read!


John D. Toner MBE L.FIHI FIHI

# Chapter 1 – Time for change

'Table' was what I heard as I walked through the door for the first time. It was a word I had heard many times with many variations; 'Away!', 'En voyage!', 'Order!', 'Go!', 'Uplift!' – so many, but they all mean the same thing, the food or meal is ready to be taken from the kitchen. Now, depending on the tone used, the person serving knew how quickly they should collect the meal from the kitchen, or they could face the wrath of said caller.

This was how I entered the place that became a life changing experience for me.

It all started a couple of weeks previously, when I decided to sell my bar, which was located in mid Wales. I had come to Wales a couple of years previously to lick my wounds after my marriage of 25 years had ended. I am honest enough to say that it was – for the most part – because of me.

My sister invited me to come over for a break, which later turned into an opportunity to re-invent myself. She is my older sister, Arlene, who is married to a Welsh man – Steve. They lived just outside Aberystwyth. She suggested I took a break just to get my head showered for a day or two, so I thought, 'OK, I will!'

Arlene is the kind of big sister everyone should have. Since losing our parents, she has always been my go to person for advice and nurture. She is level headed and very loyal. There have been times in the past when I have phoned her at 2 am, after alcohol had been consumed. Arlene would listen, give a bit of advice, then say, 'Goodnight.' Next day she would phone me – I would see her name appear on the screen, 'Aww, she is calling to check I'm ok,' I thought. Boy was I wrong! She blasted me for disturbing her house in the middle of the night!

'Now, you know I love you, Graham, but …'

Ok, I got the message, 'Sorry, sis,' I interjected.

We do laugh about those distant days now.

It was definitely a good decision to go to Wales. I arrived on a Friday afternoon a couple of weeks before Christmas, intending to stay only for a few days.

'We are going to take it easy today, but tomorrow we will go into town to see the market. Then tomorrow night we are heading to a lovely eating house for dinner,' Arlene announced.

I was happy with that plan, I was looking forward to just chilling.

On Saturday I spent most of the day just getting my bearings and familiarising myself with the town. There was a Christmas market and that certainly gave the town a beautiful vibe. I loved the fact that it was a seaside town with a great promenade, where I could sit and look out at  the vast ocean.

I got a real feeling of peace and relaxation just lazing on the seafront wall – it reminded me of Newcastle, Co. Down, a place where I spent a lot of  my life living and working,

Newcastle was where I lived when I was first married – in fact, it's where we lived right up until the youngest of my four kids turned eleven and was about to go to 'big school'. This was a time when I was happy and believed that it would be my life forever!

I did love Newcastle with its great seaside, every day – plus, I could walk out my front door,  lift my eyes and see the Mountains of Mourne right there! There was just something peaceful about living so close to the mountains and being able to walk along the promenade and sit on one of the numerous seafront benches and get lost in one's thoughts.

It's also where I first got excited about becoming my own boss, when I was working in the infamous *Royal Ascot* in Carryduff. I had started there as head chef, but after about five years I decided I wanted to open my own place. I discussed it with the owner of the *Ascot* and he introduced me to an accountant who was looking for a business partner, in the shape of a chef to open a new restaurant in Belfast.

After several meetings and listening to his desires I felt we could be a good fit, so I signed on the dotted line and parted with my hard earned savings! It worked well for a while – I ran the place, I did the hiring and firing, while my business partner ran the books and sorted out all the accounts. This system worked well until his wife saw an advert in the evening newspaper that read, 'Two hardworking students looking for work, willing to try anything.'

There were contact details listed for them. She called them and these two individuals turned up to start work in the restaurant – like two guys who didn't know the sixties were over! They hadn't shaved and were wearing unkempt clothes. Obviously, I didn't let them start – whereupon a heated discussion between us partners ensued, with him saying his wife believed she should be allowed to hire staff as he had the biggest amount of money invested.

As we continued arguing and discussing this I went and lifted a coke to drink. It was at this juncture he said, 'You didn't pay for that!' It wasn't a question, in fact it was more of a statement, with attitude.

'Oh dear,' I said sarcastically, 'I must be stealing it. Shoot me!'

I could see he was doing his best to regain the higher ground, but what he didn't know was that when we got a coke order delivered every week I would have fed the drivers and they in turn gave me a case of coke free. I always placed the case straight into the stock, which allowed me to have an odd coke when I wanted one!

Unfortunately, that particular advert and his wife's interference destroyed the working relationship and when he offered to buy my part of the business I was glad to sell! And so once again I was back to the drawing board.

One thing about being a chef is you are very rarely out of work – in fact it usually only takes one or two phone calls and you're right back in the thick of it! As it happened new owners had taken over the *Royal Ascot* and were delighted I was available. Within 24 hours I was back there as Head Chef, then two years later as owner of the restaurant.

The memories I have from my time at the *Royal Ascot* are bitter sweet! It's where I learned so much about how to run a business, but also where I learned how NOT to do it!

When we first took it over it was going well. We had maintained the level of clientele we were used to – I keep saying, 'We', and that is because there were two of us involved in taking it over. This time I was working with a long term friend, so I thought it would be different.

Like a lot of partnerships we started off great and were pleased with how it was going, but after fourteen months cracks started to appear and by the time we had hit our two year anniversary we were barely communicating. I was the major investor, so I made a lot of the decisions – sometimes without consultation.

In hindsight I can see how this would have been a bitter pill for my business partner to swallow, but truth be told, he enjoyed drinking more than me, so I honestly started to think he wouldn't notice anyway. Obviously, I was wrong!

It was around this time that I started to feel isolated. My wife was taking care of the home, which meant every night I got home she was in bed, exhausted from looking after four children. She rose early to sort out the kids and get them to school, which meant I seemed to come home to an empty house and I woke to an empty house.

It seemed that my work life was busy, my home life not so much! I missed out on a lot – as did my family – because of my work and my ambitions. I found myself selfishly flirting with the clientele. I started to believe my own hype and started to enjoy some of the attention I was receiving.

At the time we used to use models to do promotional work at the *Ascot*. Sometimes these models felt they were above the ordinary people, so part of my enjoyment was to humble them, to the delight of my colleagues – and if I am being honest it was like a game to me! On one such occasion there were six models in promoting vodka, when one of my mates dared me to embarrass one in particular.

She stood out as the leader of the pack, so to speak – nowadays it's called a prank, I think. As they were finishing up I was giving out samples of apple pie and custard, along with mini burgers, to anybody who wanted one on the way out the door.

To cut a long long story short, as the models were leaving with their noses in the air, and as they went to walk past me, I winked at my mates and pretended to trip. As I fell forwards, I threw an entire ladle of custard over the chosen leader. Immediately, I apologised and proceeded to try and wipe her down, which of course only made it worse!

She went off on one! She was so angry and all we could do was laugh – and the angrier she got, the more we laughed. She looked in the hall mirror and, after a couple of seconds, she too laughed. I took her through to the ladies changing room, professing my shock and sadness about the whole incident.

She looked at me directly and said, 'Did you do that on purpose?'

'Don't be silly,' I winked, 'that would have needed timing and a skill way beyond my capabilities.' I just smiled and offered her a drink. She said she would – after she was sorted and changed. I wish I could say that was the end of the matter, but the truth is we ended up having an affair. I convinced myself it was OK, because I didn't feel appreciated at home!

It was around this time that the powers that be started taking an interest in what we were doing and they believed we had short-changed them by not paying the correct amount of VAT! They suggested that we give them £12,000 and then we could continue trading! For some reason neither I, my partner nor my accountant agreed with their assessment so, after a number of weeks of meetings back and forward, they felt bankruptcy would be a good lesson to teach me.

On the 18th June 1985 the lesson became a reality. It was quite a sobering experience I can tell you. One thing I remember was in the time it took for me to get from the court in Belfast to my home in Newcastle, everything official that was in my name had been transferred into my wife's name – which I can honestly say did not impress her one bit! She even had to buy my half of our house – which, thankfully, my dad was able to sort the money out for!

I also believe you reap what you sow and I had been playing with fire. I felt this was the first nail in my marriage coffin, so to speak! I think that was one of the few times my humour deserted me! But, hey ho, I still had my whites and my knives, so I went back to being an employee!

In going back to work for someone else it gave me an opportunity to go to night school and learn about where I had gone wrong. I wish I could blame it on someone else, but the truth was I had dropped the ball. I was more focused on my relationship with my business partner and how to prove him wrong, than keeping on top of what was important. Because of my own weaknesses and my ego we both lost out! But I also believe everything is a learning curve and I tried hard to learn from the whole experience. I wish I could say nice things about the VAT inspector, but my conscience won't let me lie!

I think that's why I have such a fondness for Aberystwyth – it's almost a familiar feeling, even though the mountains are not the same. The seafront is not dissimilar. I do love the sea – it conjures up so many great thoughts!

Saturday night I put a bit of an effort in and dressed in a suit as we headed out for dinner. There were five of us dining – myself, Arlene, Steve, plus two of Arlene's friends.

When we got to the restaurant it was pretty busy and in full swing. We had a drink in the bar area while waiting for the menus.

'I like this place,' I said to Arlene. 'We have been here before, haven't we? But they've changed something?'

'Yes,' she said, 'they have changed the entrance.'

'Of course! I wondered why it looked so familiar on the inside.'

The waitress gave us the menus and we each decided what we would like to eat. After about fifteen minutes we were invited to go upstairs to our table. As we got to the top of the stairs I noticed another improvement – they had cut a hole in the wall so customers could see directly into the kitchen. This meant that the kitchen always had to be clean – not always easy when you are busy! You also have to curb your tongue – another thing chefs are not good at – I bet the chefs love that!

As I walked past I said, 'Good evening, chef' – but I got no response. We can't all be pleasant, can we?

As we entered the dining room to take our seats I thought, 'Ah yes, we have been here before. I remember now looking at the feature wall.'

The waitress whispered, 'Sorry about that. Chef is in a mood this evening.'

I smiled, 'Don't stress, we have all been there.'

We sat down. As our starters were served I glanced around the restaurant. I noticed there were about six tables with people seated at them – I would think, all told, about twenty six persons. We ate our starters, which were lovely.

While the waitress started clearing the plates we heard raised voices coming from the direction of the kitchen. Arlene said to me, 'I think the Chef is either under pressure, or he has had a complaint.'

'Bit harsh,' I countered, 'to assume the chef is at fault, (I nearly always don't blame the chef).

She laughed, 'Typical you – chefs are never wrong, are they?'

I laughed, 'Obviously not!'

The voices were getting louder, plus it sounded more heated, with an over use of swear words in my opinion.

I leant in towards my sister and said, 'I don't think we are going to get our main course!'

She laughed and the poor waitress looked very embarrassed. At that exact moment we heard, 'F— you! Stick it! I'm away.'

Immediately the ignorant chef was walking in a very hurried manner towards the door!

We all sat looking at one another, wondering what would happen next? We didn't have long to wait to find out. A woman in her late forties – with a striking chest on her, was the first thing I noticed! – rushed into the kitchen, followed again by raised voices. Unfortunately, we couldn't quite hear the conversation as we were too far away from the door.

Just then, out from the kitchen came a man in his thirties with long wavy hair. We noticed he was approaching tables and he seemed to be offering apologies. My heart went out to him – sometimes chefs *are* in the wrong!

He sheepishly approached our table, starting with, 'Really, we are sincerely sorry about the bad language, but unfortunately the chef …' he tapered off, not finishing the sentence. He went on to say that he was trying to phone his fellow restaurateurs in town, to see if they could lend him a chef to finish serving his customers.

He was obviously embarrassed and continued, 'Listen, we will totally understand if you want to cut your evening short, but if you are willing to wait, you can have a drink or two, or even three, on the house.'

We noticed the desperation in his voice and my sister said, 'You sound desperate?'

He responded with, 'We are – and to be honest we are doing our best.'

'How many people are left to be served?' I asked.

'There were about fourteen main courses, plus half a dozen deserts.'

I confirmed that all the ingredients were there. I stood up and said, 'Lead me to the kitchen!'

He looked at me with hope and asked, 'Are you a cook?'

'No, I'm not a bloody cook. I am a chef!'

'Oh, sorry,' he said, 'listen, if you can help …' He was holding his hands in a praying gesture.

I went into the kitchen. I took a few minutes to make sure I wouldn't make a fool of myself and familiarised myself with the equipment, then I finished the meals.

Everyone complimented the food, plus we got a good discount, which pleased my sister! It was also when I first met Heather – she was the assistant cook. Heather was a local lady who had been there since the renovations. She was what us mere mortals would call a stunner – petite, with flowing blonde hair. She had a brilliant smile, with dancing eyes. She flitted about the kitchen, effortlessly. She was obviously confident and I asked her why she couldn't finish the meals? She informed me she was not experienced enough and didn't want to ruin the restaurant's reputation. I liked her straight away and asked her if she was married? She laughed and said, 'Yes.'

'Aw, well,' I said, 'I'm still going to call you my little butterfly,' which she liked. That's what I call her still and she calls me her teddy bear, but I think that's more to do with my size!

I discovered the lady with the great chest was the owner and the man with long hair was her husband. They were a lovely couple, although I did think she would have her work cut out with him. After some discussion I was offered the job of Head Chef – which I accepted, on the understanding that I could have four days over Christmas to go back to Northern Ireland and spend time with my family.

They told me this would not be an issue as they were closed for five days over Christmas! So now I had a great job, another reason I was delighted that I came to Wales!

Over the coming days weeks and months I concentrated on building a reputation for the place – which after eight months paid dividends when we won 'Restaurant of the Year!' It definitely was one of my better decisions coming to this part of the world!

It was around this time that my sister started suggesting I date again, but I really wasn't looking for a girlfriend – after all, they were part of the reason I was in this position! So I was in no hurry to get back into the dating scene!

After a period of about fifteen months working for other people and continuing to build my reputation, an opportunity presented itself when a local bar and eatery came up for lease. Along with my sister – who was a book-keeper in her day job – we decided to go for it. We were absolutely delighted when we were successful in our attempt. So started another new chapter in my life!

We were fortunate that the community we were located in had very few secrets and – because of how my working life started here in Wales – a lot of people had heard about how I just went in and cooked the meals that night. No matter how much I tried to explain that the previous chef had all the prep done and I just finished what he started, I still got all the credit!

First thing we did after taking over was redecorate the place and introduce new menus. We went from being a two staff kitchen to employing four people for the catering side – not counting the dishwashers. I remember we were trying to find ways to promote and advertise the place, so I decided to implement a trick used by a friend of mine which impressed me: I said to my sister on the second Saturday we were open to let me know if there was anyone in the dining room who she felt would be a 'pain in the arse' – meaning a bit of a moaner!

As we were serving the last two tables she said to me that there was a lecturer on the table who wanted a steak. She said he was a real pain and liked to talk. She hoped my prank was ready! He wanted his steak cooked medium. I made sure Arlene had checked they all had enjoyed their meals. She assured me all diners were happy so I did what I do every night, I went into the restaurant and went round all the tables introducing myself and making sure everyone enjoyed the food.

When I got to his table everyone was smiling. I offered him apologies, to which he said, 'What for?'

I told him that I wasn't satisfied with the meal I had served him, so I wouldn't be charging him. He was flabbergasted, 'But it was lovely,' he said.

I said, 'Maybe, but I have a reputation to uphold. I felt I could do better.'

You could never have paid for that kind of publicity – people were talking about the Chef who actually won't charge you if he thinks it's not good enough!

Oh, don't think I never got any complaints! Every so often you would get punters trying it on, saying they didn't think it was as good as it could be (I give them credit for trying).

We were really pleased with how well it was going. We also held live music events – we had bands come from all over to perform. One of the most popular acts was, 'The Two Pats', from Birmingham. Whenever they were booked to perform the restaurant would be booked out and the bar was packed.

I would have to say they, plus a singer called 'Joey Starr', were our most successful bookings! Joey Starr was well known in Wales. He was a Welsh man with an amazing voice, who did covers as well as his own material. It never ceases to intrigue me how some people make it 'big' in the music industry, yet there are so many amazing, exceptional singers, who seem not to – although they might not see it like this, considering they are making a decent living out of performing five or six nights a week.

I thoroughly enjoyed my time in the bar, plus I got to meet some very interesting people. A number of them stood out – like the Friday afternoon club, a crowd of local guys who always came in with their boss every Friday afternoon, whereupon he would set a load of tenners on the bar and say, 'After that is gone they buy their own!'

I did laugh, because over the next four hours I heard so many great stories and we had a lot of fun. They especially liked me telling them jokes about 'the Irish man, Welsh man and English man' and, as long as I made the English man look stupid, they didn't care how funny the joke was – they laughed!

One joke in particular they loved me telling was where a Welsh man was transporting ten monkeys to a zoo, when he broke down on the motorway. As he phoned the RAC and was sitting waiting an English man stopped to offer any help he could. The Welsh man said, 'Well, you could help me. There's £50 for you if you wouldn't mind taking these monkeys to the zoo?'

'Of course, I will,' said the Englishman and loaded them into his wagon. About an hour and a half later, as the RAC man was fixing his car, the man looked across the motorway and saw the English man going past with the monkeys still on board!

'Hey!' he shouted, 'you were supposed to take them to the zoo?'

'Oh, I did,' said the Englishman, 'but we have enough money left, so I'm taking them to the cinema now!' (it was a bit funny!)

When we took the bar over it was going well. I feel we took it to another level and it is still going strong. I certainly have very fond memories of the bar and of the many customers we met.

Unfortunately, after us running it for about eighteen months the government, in its wisdom, decided to introduce the smoking ban. I felt it was going to have a big impact on our business – I wasn't wrong! I can't say I agreed with the policy at the time, although now when I go out to a restaurant, I have a different opinion.

So, with the writing on the wall, so to speak, I started looking around for other opportunities that might suit me. My background has always been in catering. From when I was nine years old I had wanted to be a chef. The reason I made this decision at such a tender age was, in truth, not for any major heart-warming reason. No, it was a much more pragmatic decision than that.

It all came about simply because of my mother. She was a force of nature and a very formidable lady, who used to watch the original, *'Crossroads Motel'* – which aired every evening on ITV just before or after the evening news. I think this was about 1964. Well, when my mum's programme was on we were not allowed to speak – or else!

My mother was a woman who deserved much more credit and appreciation from her offspring than she really got, but sadly, because of the times, and partly because of her own upbringing, mum found it challenging to express her love or emotional attachment. She had lost a couple of babies through miscarriages and stillbirth, but seemed determined to have a family which she did.

She went on to have seven children: four girls and three boys (two sets of twins – one set boys and one set girls – included in that seven). We were like stepping stones in age – from the oldest to the youngest there was only a year or so between each of us!

We thought we had it tough! There wasn't a lot of money about in those days. Dad worked as a civil servant and at the time was the only breadwinner in the family. The minute our mother thought you were old enough you were sent out to work. When I was nine I helped Mr Patterson do his milk round every day before school, for which I got seven shillings and sixpence every Saturday. Of course, that went into the house-keeping pot and all I got was two shillings!

I wasn't a bit happy about it, as it meant I had to learn how to increase my earnings. If it hadn't been for my entrepreneurial attitude …! One way I did that was to buy packets of ten cigarettes for a shilling, or one and six, and sell them as singles for threepence – thereupon I doubled my money!

Also, once a month Mr Patterson collected the milk payments and on that day I got an extra half a crown, which I told no one about. I thought I was a genius until one Saturday I took my best friend Raymond to the cinema to watch a cowboy film. I treated him to sweets, drinks and popcorn, as well as ice cream. Big mistake!

By the time he got home, Raymond was not feeling well and when he got into his house he was sick! His mum was a friend of my mum, so when she was in our house later that day she told mum all about me buying Raymond all his goodies and how he over indulged. Now, instead of sympathy, all my mum could say was, 'How did Graham afford all that?'

As soon as Raymond's mum left, the gestapo side of my mother came to the fore. She called me into the house and commanded me to stand at a certain point in the room that she could reach without much effort. 'Now,' she said, 'I am going to ask you a couple of questions and as you can see I have put the poker in the fire to get it ready.' I looked to my right and noticed the poker in the fire starting to turn red).

'So, how much money did you have this morning – considering I only give you two shillings?'

I had to think fast, which I did, and I exclaimed, 'Mr Patterson give me an extra half-crown as a bonus.'

'So, why didn't you tell me?' she said.

I whimpered, 'Because he said it was for me!'

I knew what was coming, but what kept me strong was how happy I was that Raymond was sick and how I hoped he was suffering! Thankfully, we never did get to know what mum would have done with that poker – but it certainly kept us all from telling lies!

What I mostly felt was a wooden *Schol* shoe she always used as her weapon of choice to smack us with on the bare legs – and it certainly did what it was supposed to do!

It was only after the youngest, Maxwell, started secondary school that mum got a job in the local leather factory. There might not have been a lot of money, but what we learned at that early age was that coming from a sizeable family meant there was always bloody noise, with the seven of us competing to be heard!

Of course Sandra, the eldest, thought she was an adult way before she really was. She used to continually try to control us, but she was no match for Audrey – who was originally called Avril, but didn't like that name, so changed it to Audrey.

Now Audrey was what we called a screamer and would not care who was in the house – if she couldn't get her way then she just screamed. It made the rest of us laugh, because Sandra would always be embarrassed, especially when she had any friends over. I think that's when Audrey realised that she could be rewarded for screaming, because Sandra would pay her not to – and I used to give her cigarettes to be quiet!

I must say I always felt sorry for my poor father. He was the opposite to mum. He was a hugger, affectionate, and always seemed to have time for you. He was a quiet man by nature – unless stirred, which didn't happen very often. He was hardworking in our eyes and didn't get the appreciation we felt he deserved from mum.

Every night when he came through the door he was greeted by my mum telling him to 'beat' one or more of us for misbehaving (poor dad!). On more than one occasion he would just smack us all – except, of course, his blue eyed daughter, Sandra, whom dad would never believe could do anything wrong (laughing – but we knew better, although she always got away with it)!

We were resentful of her at times but, like all families, we got over it quite quickly. Indeed, as we all got older our big sister always had real hot friends who came to the house – which was a treat for myself and Gordon ('every cloud …'). This was in spite of the fact that she behaved like a Gestapo trainee when they were there, and on more than one occasion threatened us with the dreaded poker – ha-ha, but we loved it!

On this particular evening as we were watching *Crossroads*, there was a kitchen scene in which Carlos Rafael – who was the head chef – was seen to be busy preparing for a function of approximately 50 people. In the middle of this scene the camera cut back to the reception, where Meg Mortimer (the owner) was taking a phone call from someone who wanted to change the numbers for said function. She hung up and headed to the kitchen to inform Carlos. She entered the kitchen and started to tell Carlos about the changes.

He held his hand aloft, 'Quiet,' he shouted, then told her (not politely either!) to get out of his kitchen.

As she tried to object and explain why she was there, he continued to raise his voice and repeated, 'Get out of my kitchen!'

Amazingly, she went!

I went to speak, but got that cold Scottish stare (my mum was from Scotland), which I understood to mean, 'Don't even think about speaking!' The programme ended about ten minutes later – although to my nine year old mind it was like an hour! As the credits rolled I spoke, 'I thought Meg was the owner?'

Mum said she was.

'But I thought Carlos told her to get out of his kitchen?'

'Yes,' mum said, 'that's because it's his domain and the head chef has control and power over his kitchen!'

That was it for me. I decided there and then I was going to be a chef – if only for the opportunity to throw an owner out of their own kitchen! I don't believe there is anyone else in my family, past or current, involved in catering – although my sister Audrey did work in a chippy when she was younger, but that doesn't count in my eyes.

And so it was from that young age that I worked hard at school to achieve the grades I needed to progress through to – not only Catering College, but also employment, which came at the age of fourteen. The manager of the *Slieve Donard Hotel* in Newcastle was Mr John Miskimmons – a decent man, who liked to encourage those interested in catering. I wrote him a letter telling him I wanted to be a chef and how much I would love to learn in the famous *Slieve Donard*.

It is a famous County Down hotel, built in eighteen ninety six by the then *Belfast and County Down Railway*. It took two years to complete and a lot of famous people have stayed there: including Charlie Chaplin, George Best, Robert Mitchum – along with some famous golfers. Over the years it has increased in size – partly by design, but partly by necessity, because of the troubles. It was always meant to be an hotel. It has changed hands a couple of times and is currently owned by the Hastings family (since the early seventies), but when I first started it was owned by The Grand Metropolitan Group!

They would take young people on as apprentices and train them in their chosen field. So, because I was going into the kitchen, I was told by the boss that, if I stuck at it, the hotel would pay my college fees – but for now I was a Commis Chef. They did eventually pay for my college tuition.

# Chapter 2 – New Horizons

'Excuse me!' It was one of the waitresses carrying the meals from the kitchen. I moved to let her past.

As I stood soaking up the atmosphere of the place, I found myself re-designing the interior in my mind. I could see that if the counter was moved we could make more space to allow for another table – which would mean more bums on seats, that in turn could increase turnover.

'So G, what do you think?' The question was from Pamela, the owner.

'I think it's great', I responded. 'I particularly like the ceramic on the wall' – I pointed at a feature wall, which held a large ceramic Cup & Saucer, sitting on a blue table top. It all suited the décor of *The Café Plaza*. I immediately thought of something else that would lift that wall as well.

Pamela was a woman of about twenty eight. She was about five three – an attractive lady, who on the surface seemed confident, but when we sit down to have a chat she seemed anxious. She explained to me that she was up to her neck in preparations for her forthcoming wedding, which was going to be on the tenth of May – to be precise, exactly two days after my brother's birthday, who just happens to also be my twin!

She was talking nineteen to the dozen, relaying all the positives of the business …

I held up my hand and said, 'Whoa, slow down.'

I tried to calm her down. I asked to see the account books. As I was looking over them I talked to her about the staffing levels and the wages bill? It was at this juncture she told me that one of the reasons she wanted to sell was because her husband to be had been offered a job in England, which meant it wouldn't be practical to hold onto this place.

I asked her about her staff members. I noticed there was no uniform policy – to the point that one waitress in particular stood out because of her attire. I asked Pamela, 'What's the craic with her?'

Pamela made a face, 'That girl is a nightmare employee, a good enough worker, but always sleeping in, and tardy in appearance.'

'Why don't you sack her?' I enquired.

'Because I go to church with her parents! On top of that her dad is the pastor, so it wouldn't look good.'

I laughed out loud. I couldn't believe that in this day and age someone who owned a business could be such a coward.

'If you're interested in buying *The Café Plaza*,' she asked, 'would you please take this girl on, then decide what to do with her after that?'

After some negotiations I decided to purchase *The Café Plaza*.

Pamela had mentioned how expensive her wedding breakfast was going to be, which got me thinking!

'I have a suggestion,' I ventured. 'I will cook a four course meal of your choice for your Wedding Breakfast, plus, I will give you this amount.'

I wrote down an amount on the page in front of us. 'What do you think?'

After some discussion of the wedding day meal we agreed to do a deal. The arrangement was that I would supply a soup starter, a roast beef main course, with vegetables, potatoes, etc., and a choice of two desserts, plus tea or coffee, for her wedding – as well as cash. All in all I felt it was a good deal! I was to become the new owner in the time it took to sort out the legal stuff.

As part of the original deal I was to shadow Pamela for a couple of days, but when I started unfortunately

Pamela could only give me the one day, which didn't really bother me. I am used to taking control, so it wasn't an issue for me.

So, February 20th I became the new owner of *The Café Plaza*. I was excited and nervous at the same time. I started on a Friday, so decided just to watch what happened that day and the next (Saturday) – to see how it worked.

I noticed a number of things that I was sure my experience and knowledge would improve. There were no table coverings on the tables, plus, as I said, no uniform policy! I noticed two of the waitresses wore thongs, which might be suitable attire in some settings, but not here. Also, some of the girls wore coloured bras, which in my mind looked cheap in a restaurant setting! Some wore leggings – aghh! a pet hate of mine!

There were a couple of to-do lists forming in my mind. I phoned some local trades people I knew in the area and discussed what I needed. They agreed to come in that evening to measure up, plus see what was needed – especially as I wanted the work done in two days' time. Not only that, but it all had to be completed in one day! Naturally, it would cost extra, but they could manage it.

Immediate changes were my first priority, so when we closed up on Saturday evening I informed all the staff that come Monday there would be a few surprises. I wanted them to be there at 8:15 am, which would be their new start time. I had seven girls and two blokes in my employ. Up until now they started at 9 am for a 9:30 opening, but I was going to change that to enable us to catch the breakfast crowd.

We closed on Sundays, which was why I had arranged for painters, etc. to be there to re-decorate. The joiners were in to move counters. By the time Monday morning came we had transformed the place. I changed the layout slightly and moved the counter. I introduced a complete new colour scheme. I had added, *Welcome,* in eight different languages to one of the walls, which was I felt was an inspirational thought when you consider the number of foreign students who come to the town for the university.

I also had a signature wall where people can sign their names – I had seen it once in a restaurant when I was in Canada and loved the idea. The students loved this, as did the other punters. We had a note at the top of the wall inviting them to sign their <u>name only</u>! The tables now had coverings on them and we even managed to add two tables – eight more seats! We re-vamped the toilets and put new doors on the cubicles. All in all I thought it was worth the extra money. I was well pleased.

I started preparing fresh scones, plus soups, in the kitchen – where I had knocked a wall down. I had also added a new industrial cooker, as well as redesigning the wash-up area – so the staff didn't have to walk through the kitchen to leave dirty dishes in, but instead they just set them on a counter top through the hole we had created in the wall.

As I waited for the staff to arrive I allowed myself a congratulatory moment to take it all in. It really looked different enough for me to be proud of what I had done thus far – plus I thought it made a statement that there was a new era starting, which was exactly what I wanted!

# Chapter 3 – New Day

The gasps and wows from the staff were all I had envisaged. Indeed, I had hoped they would be!

As I said good morning to all I was informed by Wilma that Phillip, the chef, was not coming in, as he was sick! I noticed two of the waitresses weren't there, either!

I looked in Wilma's direction for clarification as to why? Wilma, who up until then was a kind of self-appointed assistant manager, started voicing negative comments about the two girls, observing that this was normal behaviour, apparently. If it was up to her they should be dealt with severely, to set an example.

I let her continue for a further few seconds, then changed the topic of conversation entirely to the changes I had made. I asked for thoughts. Everyone had very positive things to say – they loved the new colour scheme, plus the wash up made more sense – everyone except, that's right, Wilma!

She thought it would make too much noise piling the dishes up, to which I asked, 'Why would they be piling up if the dishwasher is doing their job?'

She just ignored me! Wilma was in her early twenties – not unattractive, but I sensed there was something that ate at her to make her so negative. On the plus side she seemed negative about everything, so it wasn't necessarily because she disliked any one person! She had some scarring around her chin, which I assumed was a remnant from teenage acne.

I took a mental note to find out a bit about her and why a person her age felt the way she did! She always tried to sound like she had an air of authority, but sadly, I thought she was one of life's under achievers and seemed by nature to dislike change – not only about the premises, but about everything in life. It was at this point I realised Wilma was never going to like anything I would do – a moaner, the type who just sucks the life out of you. Ugh!

It was time to get started, 'Uniforms, ladies and gents! Starting today female uniform is as follows: white blouse, black skirt, flesh coloured tights, or stockings, white bra and NO thongs!'

'You can't say that to girls!' Wilma insisted.

I kept on talking, 'I can and I have! I will pay for new blouses and give a tenner towards skirts, which will be knee length, flat black shoes. We won't be opening until 10 am today to allow everyone time to go get their uniforms sorted.'

'Shiloh, as from today chef's whites will be worn while on duty, OK?'

'Yes, boss,' was his proper response.

Shiloh was like 90% of the staff – in his early twenties, not from the area originally, but had come to the university and stayed on afterwards. He had a great mop of jet black hair that you noticed immediately – as I guessed the ladies would as well – he was a good looking lad! Turned out he had come to Wales with his girlfriend, who, I discovered, was actually his childhood sweetheart – nice to know true love still exists!

I continued talking, 'From tomorrow we will be opening every day at 8:30 am to catch the breakfast crowd, which means new work patterns will be introduced.

'Also – and this is important to know – I have a 'three strike policy rule'. If, for whatever reason, you mess up three times, you're out!' (I can never understand why employers have these HR departments. who want to have meetings and discussions about employees who continually mess up, but get away with it because of HR procedure).

'What does that mean?' Wilma asked.

I quickly clarified, 'What does that mean? It means if you're late, or not in proper uniform, or do anything that goes against the company, you're sacked! End of story! OK?'

She looked bemused.

I just kept going, 'Everyone understand?' I got an acknowledging nod from all!

We opened at 10 am that morning.

The response from the public was very encouraging. I had changed the background music, which a number of people commented on. All seemed to be going well – plus we got a number of comments on our signature and welcome walls!

It was nearly noon when a sleepy, tired, 'pulled through a hedge backwards'-looking waitress appeared. She was wearing half a blouse, a screwed up cardigan, a mini-skirt, leggings, a rainbow sock roll up thing on one leg, her hair was not tidy, plus she was wearing a black bra! Agh!

I heard her mumble something to Wilma, who didn't seem to care!

I stepped in, 'Excuse me, a word please?'

I took her and Wilma into my office. 'Right you,' I said, pointing my remarks directly towards her, 'you're supposed to start at nine, not twelve?'

She humphed, then mumbled that her mum never called her …

I interrupted, 'I am not interested. I'm not Pamela – so here's what's going to happen. If you want a job here, you get here ten minutes before your shift starts. But, for now, go home, wash, tidy yourself up. Wilma will tell you the new uniform code, which I expect you to respect!'

'I don't care that your Father is the pastor. (I really didn't mean to say that, as it had no reference to the discussion). You also adhere to the three strike rule!' She just looked blankly at me. 'Be back here by 1.30 pm, or I will assume you have quit!  Now, go!'

She then left the office.

Wilma almost immediately started to run her down.

I grasped the nettle, 'Wilma, do you enjoy your job?'

'Not really,' she replied, 'I would prefer to work in an office, but I couldn't get a job. I know Pamela through our church. She needed help, so I'm here – although, if I'm honest, I think it could be run better!'

'Ok? Let's hear how you would do it?'

Poor girl nearly fainted! She responded with, 'Will I be the Assistant Manager?'

I laughed, 'Does that make a difference to your answer?'

'Well, I don't think I should help unless I'm appreciated?'

I decided, rightly or wrongly there and then, she had to go.

'Wilma, just get back to work. I will decide management structure when I see how everyone works.

'You mean you might make one of the other ones my boss?' She said it with such indignation I nearly burst out laughing in her face.

'Oh Wilma,' I said, exasperated, 'get back to work!'

We got on with lunch, which was busier than usual, or so I was told. I noticed the waitress was back, transformed and looking the part. I nodded at her, thumbs up, 'that's better' – but all I got was a look of hate.

Fun times ahead for me!

The chef, Phillip, who was normally in charge of the kitchen, never came back, so I started another chef de partie. Including myself, there were now four staff who worked in the kitchen. With current staffing levels I felt this was going to work well. The first day had been a huge success, which made me believe I had made a good move! I felt excited for what was ahead.

Over the next couple of weeks I implemented a few more subtle changes, which I thought for the most part were well received by staff and customers alike. As things progressed everyone was adapting to my management style. On the surface it seemed a happy place to work – all except Wilma, who, when-ever we had any kind of conversation, never hesitated to tell me hers was only a temporary job – she would far rather work in an office. She did make me laugh!

One particular day I had an appointment with my accountant, Ron. We were due to meet at one, but he texted saying he was running late. He arrived after two. The usual banter ensued, teasing each other. As we sat down to chat I asked him how come he was so late?

Ron explained that the last couple of weeks had been a nightmare, 'I'm two staff down in the office. Don't suppose you know anybody looking for a job? I'm looking for a couple of people to do some basic office work!

'Are you serious?' A light came on in my head, 'As a matter of fact, I actually do know someone who might be able help you in your predicament.'

I told Ron a bit about Wilma. I asked (begged) him to give her a week's trial – 'if she works out, brilliant, if not, she can come back to me.' (I'm praying now!)

I called Wilma, who looked like I was going to shoot her or something. As she came over to us I asked her, 'Who looks after you?' I say. 'I have only gone and got you your dream job!'

'Seriously?' was her excited response. She was obviously surprised. Her second thought was, 'Why? Do you want rid of me?'

I pleaded the fifth, laughing! But then, true to form she reverted back to type – the 'what ifs' started: 'What if people don't like me? What if I can't do it?'

'Wilma,' I interrupted, 'I am giving you one week off from *Café Plaza* to try it out. I will keep your job open for a week, so if you don't fit in, or like it, you can come back.

'Oh, right', reluctantly she said. 'Ok, I will do it then!'

I was delighted and genuinely hoped she would fit in there – not just for me, but as much for her herself. I thought she needed to feel accepted.

As it turned out she never started at Ron's office, because over the weekend Wilma got a job somewhere else and left! Wow! Made me wonder why she couldn't have done that sooner?

Anyway, I decided I could now restructure the staff, which I had been wanting to do for a while. One or two of them had shown natural leadership. I decided to make Glynwin a supervisor over the shifts opposite to the ones I worked, and promoted Chrissie to be our number two on whichever shift she was on. They both had the support and respect of the rest of the staff.

# Chapter 4 – Job Change

The business was starting to forge ahead well. We were maintaining a good reputation, plus a regular client base. It was after about four months that I decided to offer a Gourmet Dinner Evening the last Friday and Saturday of every month, starting end of June!

We only advertised within *The Café Plaza* and by word of mouth. I put up the menu, priced at forty pounds per person. Because we weren't licensed, we could not sell alcohol, but I could give it away, or you could bring your own.

I was hoping to be fully booked, which would be between forty and fifty diners. Plus, if we fixed up the upstairs room, we could use it as a private room for up to ten persons. The menu for our first Gourmet Dinner Night was as follows. I felt it was a good balance – especially as most of my clientele would know that all the ingredients were locally sourced, which is always a bonus.

The month of May was, of course, Pamela's wedding – which was turning into an Epic Drama, ha! In my past pre-*Plaza* days I had ran an Outside Catering Company, so I knew quite a lot about catering for special events. In fact, I used to excel at these type of functions!

What had started out – and was priced accordingly – as a four course meal was turning into an eating extravaganza. Every other day I was receiving phone calls from either the bride, or a member of the bridal party, asking could we add this or that? About three weeks before the wedding I had to call Pamela and Tom, the groom, to suggest a meeting to finalise arrangements, including the menu?

As we sat down to talk their opening sentence was: 'Is there any chance we could have a Lobster Starter, like you have on your Gourmet menu, as well as what we have decided?'

I laughed and said, 'Of course you can, but – and it is a big BUT! – we will need to sort out the extra costings. Considering when we agreed the catering for your wedding, it was based on eighty persons sitting down to a four course meal, with the main course being Roast Beef – only the numbers have now been increased to one hundred and five!

'On top of that it's been requested to have another one or two meats as an option, plus a choice of deserts – as opposed to just the original two!'

They both looked at me sheepishly and asked, 'How much extra?'

I showed them in black and white that before the lobster was added it would be approximately £700. They turned white, looked at each other, immediately saying,

'Forget the lobster! Also, is there any way we can change the menu, etc. without us having to give you more money?'

Story of my life – always someone looking something for nothing! I thought about this for a second or two, then I sold them an idea that would not only help them, but could potentially save me some money as well.

'I suggest you do a running buffet, where I lay out a long table and give you a selection of up to five meats – which includes two of them as hot dishes, like a Beef curry, or Chicken a la crème – plus salads. There will, of course, be a selection of homemade breads, obviously a good choice of deserts and, because it's a buffet, you won't need as many serving staff, so the numbers can stay at a hundred and five. So, if you're happy at that then let us agree to that!

'But' – I spoke more forcefully – 'no more changes of any kind! Agreed?'

'OK', was what they both said, apologising for all the phone calls, etc.

On the day they were both delighted. We did all that they had asked for. They had a choice of Cold Turkey, Ham, as well as Beef, plus a Hot Chicken Dish, along with a Hot Steak Casserole. They had twelve different salads, about four different breads to choose from. The desert table was a smorgasbord of choice.

# MENU

**Mushrooms Luxembourg**
(choice mushrooms stuffed with pâté, smothered in hollandaise sauce, finished under salamander)

**Seared Scallops** with brown butter and lemon sauce

**Lobster tail Cocktail**
(served on homemade wheaten bread)

**Seafood Chowder**
(served with choice of homemade breads)

**Medallions of Beef** Plaza style
(3 slices of tender fillet steak cooked to taste and served with a rich Port red wine Jus, flavoured with shallots and garden fresh herbs)

**Escallop of Chicken Nicola**
(Tender fillets flattened and seasoned, pan fried with mushrooms, pepper, onions, finished with white wine and cream, presented on a bed of rice)

**Lamb Shank**, the Irish way
(Slow cooked Lamb shank with chopped shallots, garlic, carrots, leeks, fresh herbs, tomato puree finished with a flavoured Jus)

**All served with a selection of market fresh vegetables and potatoes**

**Vegetarian Options Available** (ask your waitress)

**A wide selection of Deserts offered**

**French, or Irish, Coffee**

Because it was for Pamela, their former boss, the staff really went above and beyond to make it an exceptional day. We even got a big thank you, as well as a round of applause, during the speeches! Over one hundred more happy future customers? I love it when it all works!

We allowed a five week run up to the first *Gourmet Night*. As it came closer to the night I noticed my number two in the kitchen, Shiloh, was getting nervous in relation to the menu. He continually asked me about, 'How would we do this? How would we do that? What happens if?'

Shiloh was a nice guy – he was about twenty four and obviously came from money. His shoes cost more than my suits! He had a really nice demeanour, plus he was always pleasant to everyone. I don't think I had ever heard him raise his voice since I'd met him. He'd had the same girlfriend since secondary school, fair play to him!

Now patience was not one of my strongest attributes, so once or twice I did snap at him to 'relax, just chill out, at least until the week of the dinner' – which was still two and a half weeks away! I got a sense that he was not on board with the whole thing, plus I suspected he was maybe just not confident cooking these different types of food.

On the day of the first *Gourmet Dinner* we were booked out! There was a lot of activity – we were doing our normal day up to four, then closing the doors for three hours to let the magic happen! That was the plan but, as with every plan, you need all the elements to come together – just like a recipe actually!

One element that didn't come at all was Shiloh! He phoned in sick. I was more disappointed than surprised, if I'm honest – but now I had a decision to make. I needed help in the kitchen. I phoned a chef agency – now they could help, but they wanted a fortune for the privilege – and no-one could get to me until five thirty pm! Ah? Time for Plan B!

I phoned Carol, who helped out one day a week – normally a Monday, which was my day off, officially, but I rarely took. I cried to her (laughing).

She said, 'OK,' she would come in – yippee! But, because of how much prep that was needing done I thought I needed another pair of hands. As I stepped into the restaurant I said to Glynwin (my supervisor), 'OK, I need someone to help me in the kitchen today – who can you spare?'

'Well, I've two extra girls coming in at four – if I call them to come in at three, you can have Coreen?'

I laughed. Coreen is a great worker – a student who was saving hard for a boob job (which she eventually got). Lovely girl, but I also knew her nails were too precious, so wouldn't suit the kitchen? That's a 'No', then!

'What about Chrissie?' Glynwin offered.

Again I thought for a minute and once more discussed her as an option. Chrissie was a nice enough woman – she was the oldest employee I had, had a great sense of humour. We got on really well but, knowing her she thought she could teach me! Anyway, she felt I was offering them too fancy a meal – they should be happy with shepherd's pie, she thought! No, again!

Third choice was a charm – NOT!

'Well, that only leaves …' She pointed.

'Aw, damn!' I thought to myself, 'this is the only person who works for me with whom I've never had a conversation outside of work.'

'OK,' I said, 'tell her I would like a word.'

As she came into the kitchen I could see in her eyes she would rather be anywhere else than standing talking to me. But today was too important to be distracted by nonsense, plus she did take direction well. Since that first day debacle she has been a great worker and, in truth, a valued member of staff.

'OK,' I said to her, 'I'm sure Glynwin has explained the situation to you? I need you to help me in here. I want you to do the starters tonight. I will show you how to do them. There is a choice of three starters, so if you grab a pen and bit of paper you can write it all down as we go. I will do the scallops, so you just concentrate on the other two …'

She said, 'Can you show me how to do the scallops, as well, just in case you get busy?'

To be honest, I was genuinely impressed how quickly and easily she picked it up. She even took a picture of each one with her phone! I said, 'Very good, do it like that tonight and I will be impressed – plus, call me over if you need help. Also, continually check temperatures and keep a note of them please.'

We closed the front door at four. The two persons charged with getting the room ready were quick to start the trans-formation. With everything going well in the kitchen, the restaurant getting sorted, I started to relax slightly, which meant I could concentrate on doing what I actually enjoy – which is creating good food!

As the evening approached we were all set up. I called the staff together for a general pep talk. Everyone was well turned out. We were on top of everything, so we sat down. I gave a thank you speech to all there. I made everyone take just a few seconds, plus I made them all a non-alcoholic drink – but did promise them a proper alcoholic one later! I encouraged them to stay focussed, to help one another and to enjoy the evening – plus, be gentle towards the kitchen!

# Chapter 5 – Food always works!

When it all started I was both nervous and excited with anticipation! As we got busier I was impressed with how well my 'help' was doing. She was definitely in her element showing her artistic side, whilst plating up food that a lot of kitchens would have been proud to serve. It was everything I had asked for and more. I was genuinely delighted. What's more, I actually believed I saw her crack a smile! All in all it was a very successful event. We did 46 covers in total, with no complaints.

At the end of the evening I sat everyone down and offered them all an alcoholic drink, which everyone accepted! We just chatted about how well the evening went. I also gave special thanks to the kitchen staff and said how well they had done. To my surprise 'she' asked if I was happy with her contribution? I certainly was, to which – and this caught me – she replied, 'I really enjoy the work in the kitchen.'

She hesitated, then continued, 'If you ever need to give Shiloh time off, or need help, could I work in the kitchen?'

I think everyone in the place looked as shocked as I was feeling! I give a smile asking her, 'Are you serious?

It means you're in the kitchen with me at least five days a week,' I laughed, 'Can you handle that much?'

She said as long as she keeps learning, plus I am civil and respectful towards her.

I responded with, 'I will consider it and get back to you!'

In my head I had already decided it would be a perfect solution for me and it also meant I would have a backup if Shiloh ever decided to pull another sickie.

As it turned out Shiloh did me a favour. When he came in on the Monday he tendered his resignation, because apparently, over the weekend, he had been offered another job – which he wanted to accept. The only problem was he had to start the next day! He was full of apologies. The only decent thing I could do was wish him well and thank him. I did wish him well and told him he would be missed, which was true. So my fall-back position was being implemented a lot quicker than even I anticipated!

Tuesday I started her in the kitchen. We had a chat as I tried to break down a few barriers that seemed to exist between us. Thankfully, she was receptive to the idea.

Over the next couple of days and weeks we slowly got to a place of working well together. I must say I was loving her enthusiasm, plus she wasn't afraid to ask questions. I had said to her right from the off to get herself a notebook and write down any recipes or things she noticed. I had said that it was a great way to study and remember recipes, plus temperatures.

Wow! I noticed one day she had two, maybe three, note-books. I said to her, 'Hey! Are you writing down every flipping word I say?'

She was laughing (something I had not seen her do too much before). 'Well, what I'm doing is as I see you making meals I try to remember all the key ingredients. I scribble them down quickly, then when I get home I write them out properly – plus how you cook them – into this book' – whereupon she produced another book.

She handed it to me to look at. I was genuinely impressed. It contained about thirty or forty recipes, all neatly written! I was honestly impressed. I looked at this girl in a whole new light. I acknowledged this and told her how sincerely awestruck I was. She had even commented on my knife skills – which as a chef delighted me (I know, I'm a show off!)

I thanked her for the change in attitude. She, in turn, thanked me for giving her a second chance, as she knew that when I took over she had no enthusiasm to be there. She knew she didn't show Pamela proper respect. She also knew how her demeanour had been all wrong. She went on to tell me about herself.

She was the oldest of three children – brought up in America, not far from the 'Big Apple'. Being the product of a pastor sometimes presented problems that her peers didn't have to deal with. 'Don't get me wrong,' she said, 'I know he loves his family, but it's not always as easy or delightful as people think.'

She wanted to have her own identity, so when the family came to live in Wales a number of years previously, because of her Father's work, since living here she has found her own identity. Just under a year before she'd made the decision to move into an apartment (flat) of her own – although living on her own still meant she needed her mother to wake her most mornings! This made me laugh.

'I know,' she said, 'but I'm just not good with getting up early!'

Her ambition had always been to get involved in an industry where her artistic nature could shine. I think she would shine in the fashion industry, but she enjoys that as a hobby. One of the reasons she loved the kitchen was she could use that skill when decorating plates with food, or even cakes and pastries.

We sat there talking for about one and a half to two hours. To be truthful I came away with a whole new perspective about her. I even found myself liking her

American accent. I had never heard her talk so much in one day!

Over the coming days I started to look at her in a totally different way. We started to become friends. I would have to say it was a joy to go into work every day to a happy kitchen, plus as the old adage goes, 'happy staff, happy customers, better productivity'. It went on like this for a number of weeks.

Another plus was I am someone who likes music. I have a very eclectic taste – first thing I do when I walk into work is turn on either the radio or CD player. I have a great selection of CDs and never once did I hear her suggest we change the CD, or change the station, and I even heard her sing along!

I had started a 'thing' within the church I attended of inviting up to sixteen to eighteen people to my house every other Sunday for lunch, after the church service. There were rules of course – I love curve balls – three in total to the lunch invitation: you come hungry, you do a party piece, but more importantly don't say you'll come if you don't intend to.

What had started as a way to meet people was turning into a bit of a gold ticket event, with people actually asking could they come because of all the craic there was to be had. I had a list of people who were hoping for an invite because they had been told how much fun it was when you go!

This was something that had been going on for about four months. I saw it as a twofold thing: one, it was a great way to meet people – not only that but those who came on a Sunday would usually be more receptive to using *The Café Plaza* through the week, which was of course my primary source of income – so therefore win, win. Although more than anything was when the party pieces started – the craic was ninety!

It always reminded me of when myself and my siblings get together. We all love each other dearly, but boy sometimes the noise level is something else, as we try and grab each other's attention while we are all talking at once – great memories indeed!

Anyway, my assistant cook asked if she could help me out the next time I was having one? I said, 'Yea, sure, but you know the rules?' I reiterated them, to which she replied, 'OK, as long as I can bring one of the other girls (waitresses) with me for back up and we can do something together? I laughed and said, 'Sure why not?'

It also meant I could cancel two of the casuals I normally booked and paid to help with setting up, serving – plus the one job I hate doing, washing up and putting everything back to normal. I was fortunate that the house I rented was a three bedroom bungalow with a large sunroom. The sunroom was where I held the lunch parties. It had an extending table that when opened out could seat twenty two. Of course I had to borrow some chairs from work – as well as plates, glasses, cutlery etc. – hence one of the reasons I just did it every other Sunday. This allowed me to relax properly on alternate weekends.

As Sunday came around I checked that all those I had invited knew my address and confirmed numbers. It turned out that on her first day of helping me I had also invited her parents, which I thought was a good thing! Sometimes – just sometimes – I get it wrong!

To my surprise 'she' was not too happy that Mum and Dad were going to be there. It meant she couldn't relax. I felt a bit of tension in the air. Of course I didn't know why then. I was to find out later that they had had a heated discussion about her coming to my house and how it looked to people – because I'm older than her father. Of course, had I known all this I would have confronted the issue at the time, because then it was only a boss-employee situation and totally platonic.

We got through the afternoon without any blood being shed, happily enough – plus everyone did a turn. Her Dad read a poem and her mum did some origami, which did impress. She, along with the other waitress, Ciara, did a dance routine, which Roger found Very Interesting! He said to me later it made him wish he was forty years younger again. Behave!

I really did enjoy those Sunday afternoons when people who seemed so genteel and churchy were only too delighted to show off and make fools of themselves. Sometimes you discovered they have a skill that you would never have associated with them! I had trumpet players show off their skills, singers, poetry readers, wannabe magicians. We had talks on animals, flowers … once we had a Yoga lesson while the person was dressed in their Sunday best, lol! We certainly did have some amazing fun times.

I remember one time I had a knock on my front door – it was a Wednesday afternoon. There were two Mormon missionaries standing there. They offered to cut my grass just as an 'offer of service'. I said, 'Hey, work away. I don't like cutting grass, so of course you can, as long as you let me invite you both to lunch next Sunday as a thank you. I explained the format to them and they genuinely seemed excited about the prospect.

So they cut my grass and the following Sunday they came for lunch. They told all present that they were from Utah in the USA. They were in training – part of their training involved going to another country with little money and doing exactly what they were doing, which is knocking doors offering to do chores for people just as a way of service and not looking to be paid. They did accept a drink, or bite to eat, but not cash. I did admire these two guys. Not surprisingly they commented that this was the best feed they had had in about three months! When it came time to do their party piece one asked if he could sing a hymn?

'Of course,' I said, 'it's your spot – do whatever you want.'

'Do you have a keyboard? he asked.

'I do,' I replied, whereupon I went to fetch it.

As I set it up for him he was talking with his prayer partner. I noticed they seemed to be disagreeing on which hymn to sing. Next thing the other one says, 'This is a private event and you are all church-going people? Like, there will be no one offended?'

We all nodded in the affirmative.

'There's no judgement here,' we said. I was thinking he maybe hadn't a great voice and was worried we might laugh – but that was not our style, so I encouraged him to relax and assured him he was free to be himself! With that he and his friend started.

Wow! We were shocked. They only started singing Gerry Lee Lewis', *Great Balls of Fire.* Well, we laughed.

That afternoon we witnessed two young men having freedom and fun – they even whipped off their ties to treat us to a dance routine! They certainly gave us a great concert, making it a brilliant afternoon, which, had we videoed it, I think I could have made a fortune through bribery! Also, I did invite them back through the week for tea and we got to know each other quite well over a couple of months. They performed a couple of times for the Sunday group. I was sorry to see them leave when it was time for them to go back home to America.

There were usually about twenty to twenty two persons in total there. I always invited a couple of men from the weekly prayer group I was attending every Monday night. Roger always came – he was a man about twelve years older than me. He was about six foot four inches tall, from the Midlands. Roger was a striking looking man, with an accent I just loved. His party piece was he had a hankering to be a comedian. Boy, we really laughed at him trying to tell jokes where he continually had to change key words to make the jokes more church-friendly. Ha-ha, we could see him struggle, which give the whole performance so much more hilarity. Roger had been married and divorced a couple of times, but he had a heart for people. He had a great baritone voice, but he wouldn't sing on his own! I loved this guy and we are still very close to this day, even though we have a vast pond between us.

There were always ten to twelve men at our Monday meeting. Apart from Roger, there was Stephen, a lovely guy with an amazing past. This man had lived through a lot that I think would have broken most people, but his faith had sustained him. I was always amazed at just how gentle he was and never showed any kind of bitterness.

Then there was 'two tents' – a man of the cloth. I nicknamed him 'two tents', because once, while we were discussing about having a weekend away, someone suggested camping. 'Ha!' I laughed out loud (because there was NO way I would be camping), when the vicar said, – a bit louder than he needed to – 'I've got two tents.' And because he said it aloud we all stopped and looked at him a bit surprised, as he is normally quite a humble man. As we sat looking for a second or two I interjected with, 'OK, big boy, no need to boast!' We all laughed and he followed up, almost embarrassed, 'No, oh sorry, I just remembered.' he said.

We had some great nights with powerful prayer times at those Monday night meetings. That's where I met a solicitor, a plumber, a painter (artist), accountant – there was a real mix of occupations and ages. One man in particular I had a real fondness for was Arthur. He was a man of advanced years – eighty plus – but he was as fit as a butchers dog – still cycled and walked every day. But his most endearing quality (not everyone liked it) was his honesty and directness. He had no filter, he didn't care. How we laughed with him.

I remember on one occasion the visiting bishop came to one of our meetings. As we were having a tea break the bishop said to him, 'So, you enjoy cycling, then, Arthur? How far would you cycle every day?'

'Oh,' says Arthur, 'I go up and down the promenade a couple of times when the sun shines.

'You like the fresh air, then? the bishop said.

Laughing, Arthur replies, 'No! I like to look at the girls in their bikini or bra tops – keeps my blood pumping!'

The poor bishop was flummoxed, but we all loved it!

It was on one of these Monday nights when one of the men gave me a gentle warning. Every week one of the staff made tea or coffee at the start of the evening. I usually had a tray of sandwiches, or buns, ready in the kitchen. This particular night Coreen was supposed to make the coffee, etc., as per rota, serve us, then head off – but apparently she got a phone call, which meant she had to leave early, so had asked the cook if she would do it for her, to which she had said, 'Yes.'

When everyone had arrived she brought out said coffee and food. As she was serving us all the men commented on how good she was. They said to me, 'What do think of her?'

'I replied, humorously, 'Oh, she is amazing, absolutely brilliant!

I thanked her. I motioned to her, 'Just leave the keys beside the till, thanks. I will see you in the morning.'

Now, most of the men's group, myself included, are huggers. As she went around the group she was hugged by most of the men. I don't usually hug my staff, but whilst I was still sitting pondering, she bent down, kissed me on the cheek, hugged me, smiled and said, 'Good night. God bless.'

I was a bit taken aback by it. We proceeded with our night. As we were preparing to leave, Noah, one of the men whom I really respected, pulled me to one side and said to me, 'Listen, G, watch yourself with that girl who served us tonight.'

I laughed, 'What do you mean?'

He said, 'I get the sense she likes you and I don't mean as just a boss.'

I asked him if he was mad, 'She is half my age! She wouldn't be interested in me romantically.'

I was genuinely surprised by him saying this! He said to me just for me to be aware of how I behaved around her.

# Chapter 6 – Changes

Next morning I opened up as normal at about six forty five am. Usually, the staff turned up at eight in time to open the doors at eight thirty am. Well, everyone turned up as per rota time – except one person!

I was surprised, to be honest, because the last four and a half months she had been brilliant, so this was unexpected. Anyway, I got on with setting up for the day ahead. After nearly two hours my annoyance turned to anger. I told the other girls there to phone her, but no luck. After four hours I started to feel a bit concerned – I mean, who sleeps in over four hours, thirty minutes late?

Next thing the kitchen door opened. It was her mother. I had noticed before that her mother was a very attractive lady. I would guess maybe about nine years younger than me. My friends would probably say she is my type – she is about five foot five inches tall, slim, with dirty fair hair and a smile that could melt hearts. As I started listening to her it came to my mind how much her daughter looked like her!

Anyhow, she started up with apologies, saying how it was mostly her fault because she had a fall out with her pastor husband, so had gone to her daughter's flat with two bottles of wine to drown her sorrows. It was nearly four am before they got to bed – hence the sleeping in – and now her daughter was really upset, concerned for her job.

To be honest, part of me was relieved to know she was OK! My anger had been replaced with genuine concern, but I now had to put on my boss's hat, which I did. I asked, 'Where is she, now?'

Mum told me she was outside in the car, waiting to find out if she still had a job?

'Well, firstly this is a conversation for her and I to have, not me and you,' I smiled politely. I told her sarcastically to behave, send her daughter in, 'Who I believe is an adult?' I snickered, mother smiled. Damn she was a fine looking woman!

Her daughter came in very sheepishly. If I was being honest, I didn't know if it was because of what Noah had said the previous night or because of her mother, but all of a sudden I saw a woman walk in.

She had features similar to her mum, as I said, but her hair was jet black, which flowed half way down her back. Her eyes were striking. I was really looking. I realised she was quite a stunning young lady. She was about five foot seven inches tall, high cheek bones, beautiful green eyes and a smile that showed a mouthful of brilliant white teeth. I'd always noticed that amazing smile. I would say she had a chest of about thirty eight inches, a waist of about twenty eight inches, with hips to suit.

I never before looked at her as a 'woman', but for the first time I really noticed how her eyes shone, how her smile was so brilliant – wow, she could have advertised toothpaste with that smile. It wasn't hard to understand why her body was so well toned and almost athletic looking, considering she jogged about two miles every day. I really had to steel myself to be annoyed to enable me to give her a rollicking. I didn't go over the top – I didn't really need to express my temper. She knew me well enough to understand!

I just told her that was her second strike – that no matter how much I valued her work that she could be replaced. I knew she was upset with herself. She also knew she would have to rebuild the trust. She hoped I would forgive her. She ended our conversation with, 'Am I still OK to help you this coming Sunday?' I wasn't expecting that – it definitely caught me off guard. I swallowed and quipped, 'As long as you don't sleep in?' I winked. She gave me a smile that just got me right there!

I decided to take a half day, telling her my nerves were shattered. So I left her to work the rest of the day.

As it happened, a couple of days later I had booked a trainer to come do some training on Customer Relations with all the staff. On the course the trainer, whose name was May, paired everyone off in couples, calling us married work couples. And, of course, *we* were paired as 'work husband' and wife, to which everyone laughed. I did see the humour in it!

It was an interesting day, especially having to call her 'wife' the whole time. We did enjoy the craic all the same. Over the ensuing weeks we'd see each other almost every day, plus every other Sunday. On one of those Sunday's she arrived a bit despondent.

I asked, 'What's wrong?'

She told me her TV had broken down – as well as that her sister had borrowed her DVD player, so she was just looking at the walls. I said, 'That's not a problem. Sure, if you want you can come round to mine anytime – to watch TV, or a video – 'I'm out four or five evenings a week, anyway.'

She was really appreciative. At the start it was once or twice a week, but after a couple of weeks it became more often. Occasionally, we would sit talking for hours about ourselves and our lives – I told her about my life, my history, about my family. She in turn told me about hers – about her growing up just outside the Big Apple, about the big factory in her town, about her grandparents, about her sister and brother.

She told me about the obstacles she had endured growing up, because her Dad was a pastor – oh, she loved him and her Mum deeply. She just felt slightly restricted, unable to blossom as an individual. She had a passion for design, art – plus the written word. I remember more than once catching her reading a book with tears rolling down her cheeks – she could become so engrossed in the story she could feel the pain of the characters she was reading about!

One particular night I remember we were just sitting relaxing, I found myself looking at her. I noticed that when she laughed her whole being seemed to dance in time with every sound that she made.

Whoa, come on man. STOP! I realised that I was finding myself actually having feelings for her. I also realised my nights out were no longer a priority for me. I immediately stopped myself from thinking in this way. I decided to try and change the dynamics of this friend-ship! 'Methinks I need to upgrade the menus in work', which meant I would have to stay in work in the evenings to test new recipes for the menu.

In effect, it curtailed the amount of time we were spending together. This was only going to work for a while, but I needed to get her out of my head – after all she was half my age. She was only twenty six! Damn it I was fifty four!

It was around this time I started someone else to help in the kitchen. His name was John. He was going to do three or four afternoons a week, so I could finish around two thirty, after lunches, because I start most mornings about six thirty. I liked to get away early doors!

John was semi-retired. He was just looking to do twelve to sixteen hours a week, so it wouldn't affect his benefits. It suited me down to the ground. Also in his favour was the fact that he did things the way I liked them to be done! He was a single parent. He had lost his wife to cancer six months ago. He was still in mourning, plus was trying to stay strong for his three young kids. John was one of the good guys. He came in, did his work and went home – no dramas!I respected him greatly, but he wasn't ready or looking to make 'new' friends, so it stayed a work only relationship.

This work pattern was working well for about two weeks, but then after just two weeks one Tuesday afternoon she was on a half day. She had left work by the time I finished at three pm. I drove down home and was in the house about fifteen minutes when I heard a knock and when I opened the door all I heard was the New York twang say, 'Hi.'

I naturally responded, 'Yoho, lovely.' I held the door open wide and motioned her in. I followed her. I said, 'Well, what's happening?'

'Nothing,' she said, 'I was just bored and was wondering if it's OK to watch a movie here?'

'Yeah, sure,' I said, 'work away.'

'Do you want a drink or anything before I start it?' she asked.

'No, I'm fine thanks, pet.'

About five minutes later my doorbell rang. I got up and went to answer the door. I was a bit surprised when the man at the door said he wasn't looking for me, he was actually looking for her! I called her to the door. I left them talking. I went into the kitchen to get myself a glass of water. After I had drunk it I set the glass down. I was heading back to my office, but as I was coming through the hall from the kitchen I saw her pulling on her boots and reaching for her coat – but wait, she was crying! Whoah!

'Hey, what's wrong?' I asked.

She hesitated, then said, 'It's OK. I have to go and see if I can find my Mum or Dad.'

'Why? Has something happened,' I asked. I could see she was not only crying, but I sensed she was embarrassed.

At that moment I realised I had deep feelings for this girl! I took control of the situation. I said, 'OK. STOP! Exactly what's wrong?'

She said, 'No, it's ok. I will sort it.'

At that point the man interjected with, 'I will give you a lift, so I can collect it.'

Again I said, 'STOP! Tell me what the issue is.'

I closed the door over, when the man put his foot in the door to stop it closing!

'OK,' I emphasised, 'my house, my door, move your foot, NOW!'

He wisely removed his foot. I stood in front of her and said, 'Right! Enough, tell me what's going on, NOW!'

She took a second to catch her breath, then told me. Apparently she was three hundred pounds in arrears with her rent and the man at the door was trying to collect it!

I said, 'Is that all it is?'

As she nodded I almost burst out laughing, but I didn't.

She said, 'I'm going to see if Mum or Dad can lend me it. He says they might throw me out if it's not sorted today!'

'Right,' I said, 'Where are the letters they sent you?'

She looked puzzled.

I said, 'Surely they have given you a warning about the situation?'

'No', she said, 'I didn't even know how much the total was till he just told me. I knew I owed some, just not how much.'

I clarified they definitely had not informed her either verbally, or otherwise, about how much rent she owed. She shook her head, 'No.'

'OK,' I said, 'take your coat off, stop crying and I will sort this.'

I opened the door and said to the bloke, 'Show me the account you're looking to collect for.'

He said rather rudely, 'Look, it's three hundred pounds!'

'Brilliant! Show me proof. Show me a breakdown of rent arrears, etc.?'

'Listen,' he said, 'it's nothing to do with you. It's between me and her. Can I at least come inside till we get this sorted?'

'No! I don't want you in my house.'

Sometimes, when you're six foot one and have an aggressive attitude it can work in your favour, as it did that day (normally I'd have let Gordon do the fighting, like when we were at school, but he wasn't there!).

'No proof on you how much is owed?'

'Not on me,' he said. 'But it is three hundred pounds.'

'Right, do you at least have a receipt book on you?' I ask.

He nodded.

'OK. If I give you money to sort this she gets a receipt?'

You could see the excitement in his eyes – he thought he had won and he was going to get all the money owed. I put my hand in my pocket. I pulled out a couple of hundred quid. His eyes lit up because he thought I was going to pay it all! I took two twenty pound notes as well as a ten pound note out of the money in my hand.

As I held it out to him I said, 'Give me a receipt for that and we will call into the office on Thursday to sort the rest out. When we get there I will be expecting – NO, demanding! – an apology from you. Coming to my door in such a menacing manner, with no evidence of who you are. Demanding money from a vulnerable young lady.'

He handed me the receipt and I told him to piss off!

I closed the door, turned around and looked at her, but before I could speak she fell into my arms. I felt her body close to me, her tears on my cheeks, breathing on my neck as I went to pull away. We looked at each other, then she just lifted her head slightly and started kissing me!

I remember once watching a film where when the lead actors kissed it showed two trains colliding – well, that was what this kiss was like. I can honestly say I had never experienced a kiss like it before. Her lips were soft and moist. They tasted a bit salty from the tears. We kissed for about two minutes. We were definitely hungry for each other. I couldn't believe how much I had wanted this.

The other thing I noticed was I didn't need to bend my head – she was the perfect height for me. Twice I tried to slow it down, but in those two minutes she was in control – not only was I a willing participant, but the intensity of it took over.

Eventually, our lips separated. We just stood there looking at each other. She knew I wanted her. While she still had her arms around me we started moving towards my bedroom. As we got to the bed and we started undressing each other I forced myself to stop. I held her at arm's length, 'Are you sure you want this to happen? (all the while praying it would).

'More than you will ever know,' she replied!

We were in bed from about three forty five until nine pm – when we were both hungry for food. I can honestly say it was one of the best evenings of my life. What lacked in experience was made up for with youthful exuberance and enthusiasm. I ordered a Chinese. After we had eaten we went back to bed. We continued getting to know each other intimately!

We played music. I have a very eclectic taste in music – turned out she loved my choices as well. I have everything from Roger Whittaker to Led Zeppelin, but one of her favourites was the Beatles! Everything seemed like a perfect fit. We talked for hours. It was while we were talking that she said to me that she had been worried I had gone off her, as she had noticed a change in me over the last two weeks.

I asked what did she mean? She said wee things like I didn't offer to give her a lift home, or didn't watch a movie with her. I seemed to be working longer hours.

I was surprised. I thought I had been more subtle. I said it was just because of the menu changes, etc.

'Anyway,' I said, 'Why would it really bother you?'

Then she said, 'Of course it bothered me. The truth is, she said, 'I have strong very strong feelings for you. I think I love you. I have done for weeks. It was killing me to think you might not like me, even as a friend, and to be honest part of the reason I had come down today was to try and talk to you about it. But then that knob head appeared.'

I looked at her deeply, 'Wow,' I said, 'that's a big statement to make. Are you sure you're not just infatuated with me as some kind of father figure?

She looked at me with a steely stare and said, 'I can assure you I don't have daddy issues and my feelings are not infatuation! They are real!'

I looked at her for what seemed like forever, then I just start speaking, saying, 'To tell you the truth,' I took a deep breath and admitted, 'I have been fighting those same feelings, because I also have them for you. That's why the last two weeks I have been the way I have been. After all this is not what you call a normal situation, plus,' I added, 'I just wasn't sure if it is because I am a sexy beast, with looks, personality, plus I'm an amazing chef, whose knife skills you admire?'

She added, mockingly, 'Some of what you just said has some merit!'

I tried laughing, but I just couldn't seem to make the sounds! 'I have to be honest, I am over the moon at this very minute. I really pray this is real and I won't wake up to discover it's all a dream!'

'Oh, it's not a dream,' she said. We both laughed and just embraced.

# Chapter 7 – New Beginnings

She never went back to her flat again – except to collect her 'stuff'. It also turned out she only owed two hundred and twenty pounds rent arrears – plus, because I complained loudly enough, she received a discount for clearing the arrears!

We wanted to keep things real so decided to keep our relationship as normal as possible – because we both knew it would be seen by everyone as just a sex thing, with me as the instigator. Although, much as I welcomed what was happening between us, I sometimes wondered who was the main protagonist.

I loved this girl's mind as well. We had some interesting conversations about everything from our ages to the Lord. She had an enquiring mind, with a desire to increase her knowledge – probably one of the reasons she also loved books.

We had discussed telling her parents about us. I said I was quite happy to tell them, but she asked me to let her tell them. Her grandfather, who lived somewhere in Switzerland, was coming to visit in a week or two. He would be staying for a fortnight, so she asked if I would mind if we left it till after they returned home?

'Of course not, no worries.'

Her grandfather is a renowned Christian genealogist and a genuinely interesting man. Because this trip coincided with one of my gourmet nights it seemed only natural for her family to book a table for dinner, which is exactly what they did.

When they arrived her Mum stuck her head into the kitchen to say, 'Hello.' As she did I was showing her daughter how to make a rose out of a tomato and obviously flirting with her, when her Mum said, 'You know, I think you two act like an old married couple.' We both looked at each other and laughed nervously.

After all the meals had been served and patrons were on their coffees I did my usual walk around, checking everyone was happy with their meals, etc. I left her family's table to last so I could spend a bit of time chatting and getting to know them. Her Grandfather was not just a professor, but a real gentleman, a lovely person. Her Nan was equally engaging. Mum introduced me as her daughter's intended. Everyone laughed except me. I smiled and acted professional – after all they're paying guests!

Her Grandfather and I got on well. We actually met up a few times for a coffee. One particular evening we went for a meal. I found him a very likeable man, whose company I enjoyed. In some ways she reminded me of him. I could see where she got her gentleness from.

He was about my height, distinguished, slim, carried himself well. When he spoke he didn't speak arrogantly, but with an unforced confidence. He asked me quite casually over dinner, 'Are you and my granddaughter having a relationship? Before you answer,' he said, putting his hand up to stop me answering, 'I don't want to put you in a position where you feel the need to lie, so let me say this, if you are I would just ask you to treat her respectfully and encourage her to let the family know, because they already believe you are!'

With that he changed the subject totally. In that moment I thought to myself, no more waiting. It makes this whole thing appear like it is some seedy affair, when in fact it's anything but! Part of me was embarrassed. It was a feeling I hadn't felt since I was a child, when I did something wrong and my father would look at me with that knowing look. I would have sensed his disappointment – not a nice feeling and not a pleasant memory.

She decided to tell her family the very next day, which I was glad to hear, although it came as no great surprise to them, apparently. In fact, they were very accepting of us as a couple – at least on the surface. Her sister thought it was hilarious, saying we were like Celine Dion and her husband. There is a big age difference there!

So almost immediately we seemed to be accepted as a couple, which had me thinking, what was her reluctance to tell them about us?

'Ah!' she informed me, 'don't be thinking that what you just witnessed is acceptance, it's not. It's called tolerance and it's just for now!' She smiled like she knew something I didn't, but I decided to let it go for then, knowing I would want to know more later.

Turned out I got an opportunity to introduce her to my siblings before anyone else. My youngest brother, Maxwell, had a son getting married in two weeks so we – well, I was – invited to said wedding. I could bring a plus one – 'Yay, brilliant!' Plus, it was in a classy place.

Maxwell was the baby of our house. My parents had a number of children – sadly, they lost a couple – but there were seven surviving children. There was Sandra, the eldest, then Arlene, followed by two sets of twins – myself and Gordon, then Alison and Audrey. Then, last but definitely not least, there was Maxwell.

It's true what they say, the baby is always the spoilt one. As I have mentioned before, while growing up we were not a rich family. Once you were old enough to earn money you got a job to help contribute to the upkeep of the house, whether you wanted to or not. Now, because Max was still at school when they were introducing school trips and adventure holidays for his year, he of course got to go – not a bit jealous, ha! Plus, because he was the baby, the rest of us – willingly, I might add – helped pay for his excursions. We called him the baby, but he stands six foot three and looks anything but a baby – although his wife might not agree, ha-ha!

We think it was because of those school trips that that's where he got the bug to travel – so, when he was old enough he joined the Royal Air Force and stayed with them for the next thirty two years, reaching the senior rank of Chief Tech. The boy has done good, plus he has travelled the world.

He left school with few qualifications, but has since gone on to gain a couple of degrees – one from the Open University, plus a Master's in Clinical Engineering, which makes the rest of us very proud. It would certainly have made our parents proud.

One good memory I have of Max is when he first joined the Royal Air Force – Max insists we use all three words. We were all working in our own jobs and earning a wage. Well, for my birthday the first year he was away he sent me a birthday card with five pounds in it. I remember saying to my dad, 'Wow! Maxwell must be doing well. He sent me a fiver!'

Whereupon my dad laughed, 'A sprat to catch a mackerel,' he said.

'What does that mean?' I asked.

'Well, it's his birthday in June so he assumes you will do the same and send him one.'

We both laughed. I never did send him a fiver and he still talks about it today – thirty plus years later – but we still laugh. Max is married to Elizabeth and they have three sons. Neil, their second eldest boy, was getting married to his childhood sweetheart – a girl called Joanne, a real star.

The wedding was a rare occasion for the siblings to all come together, which in itself is a sight to behold. When all us siblings get together it's like we have never been apart, we still each one of us try and out shout each other and try to grab the attention. It's our families I feel sorry for – they become onlookers to a chimpanzee party, ha!

It was also an excuse for my beloved to get a new dress. That turned out to be an event in itself – trying to get a dress. We were both fans of *Pretty Woman* – the film – so she asked me to go with her to purchase one, which I was only too delighted to do.

I said, 'Let's pretend I'm Richard Gere and you're Julia Roberts?'

We went into a dress shop where we were about to start our acting, when the lady in the shop said, 'Oh, hello you two. How's things?'

She knew us. It burst our bubble, so we burst out laughing. I did tell her what we had intended, and at least she laughed with us. She then asked how she could help.

I said, 'We are looking for a nice dress, size ten or twelve?'

My girlfriend gasped and said, quite annoyed, 'I am not that big! I only take a four, or maybe a six.'

Now I never like to put anyone down, but I laughed. 'If you're a four, or a six, then I am Richard Gere!'

She seemed really offended, 'Do you really see me as that big?'

'What are you talking about?' I enquired.

Now it was the turn of the shop owner to laugh. She interjected with, 'You are both right.'

I looked puzzled.

'Well, she said, 'You're talking English sizes, but don't forget your lady friend is talking American sizes, am I right?' she said. She was, so we all had a giggle.

She did get an amazing looking dress and it was a size twelve, so I won, ha-ha! Unfortunately, only myself, Gordon and Audrey were able to make the wedding, which was being held at Thornton Manor – a class establishment (apparently one of the Man Utd footballers held his reception there).

We were made to feel welcome from the minute we drove into the car park. There was someone there to greet us and give us directions to the hotel. We met up with Gordon and Fiona, plus Audrey, who was on her own.

Audrey is an acquired taste – a real special vintage. She lives in the Isle of Man and always attends family events. She likes to think that since our parents are no longer with us it's up to her to constantly remind us that she was our mum's favourite daughter. We do laugh – it wasn't true, but we don't have the heart to spoil her illusion.

Audrey has a warm heart towards anyone connected to the family and that includes girlfriends, wives, even their exes. She doesn't mind if you're separated, or even divorced – when you're in, you're in forever. We do love her.

She has some medical issues, which include an over active thyroid, coupled with problems with her legs. The poor woman is like a walking chemist – a warning though, if she was to ever offer you a lift I would advise against it, ha-ha! We don't know how she makes it from A to B – her driving is seriously flawed – but, hey, don't hold it against her! She has never had an accident, or even a dent in her cars – so she tells us!

My son in law tells a great story of how Audrey was once giving him a lift to the airport, when he says he heard the parking sensors on the front of the car sounding. Ha-ha! He says he was close to needing a change of underwear by the time they got to the airport!

Anyway, she was delighted to meet my girlfriend and almost immediately invited her to come visit her in the Isle of Man. I laughed and tried to save her. I know my sister and she could talk for hours!

A thing I like about family events is the reality of those there – they tell it like it is. There are no airs or graces there. Everyone there accepted us as a couple, with only one exception. We were made to feel like we belonged. It warmed both our hearts to feel that kind of love and affection. I know it certainly made her feel special, which is exactly what I wanted her to feel.

As I said 'one exception', but I understood the reasoning behind her attitude. I had at one time been 'friendly' with her and she felt snubbed. We did go on to have an amazing day and like most family weddings there was plenty of drink consumed and the singing was as bad – or as good – as it should be!

It happened there was an opportunity to tell my whole family at once. The occasion was to be my son's thirtieth birthday back in Northern Ireland. I was to be a 'surprise' guest and I could bring a plus one, yay! So I told my sister and my friends to say nothing to any of my lot when they came over – as I aimed to tell them the following month when I went over for Lee's birthday party – so August was to be the big 'reveal'!

The following weekend my daughter, granddaughter, as well as my sons, were over for a visit. I loved it when they all came over – we always had a party in the bar I had owned.

The current owner used to be one of my chefs – a good guy who was also a great singer. He and I used to enjoy some great karaoke nights together in the bar. When I was considering selling the bar he asked would I be willing to sell to him? I recall saying to him, 'As long as you give me money, I will, ha-ha!'

Well he gave me money and I sold it to him, but I continued to socialise there, as it has a great atmosphere, along with a pool table!

Now to date my family still didn't know my relationship status, so I thought I would have a bit of fun at their expense. Whenever they all came over together we usually went for an early evening meal, then headed up to the bar for a shindig and a night's craic.

In order for me to take my significant other I devised a cunning plan – I told her to just play along!

When Nicola – my daughter, who is an amazing, intelligent girl, has been the apple of my eye since her birth and who is also the boss in our family (we sometimes laugh at how much she reminds us of our mum) – came into the kitchen, along with Rebekah (Ba, my firstborn granddaughter), we did our hellos. Then I sat Rebekah, who was only four or five years old at the time, at a table with a colouring book and of course I got my 'assistant cook' to help her!

Rebekah thought she was just brilliant – which I knew she would, as she loved art – plus it meant myself and Nicola could catch up on all the news from home. 'Time flies' and without even realising it we had been talking for ages. Nicola said she was hungry, so I suggested we went across the street to Witherspoons for a curry, especially as I do love their korma.

She said, 'Let me get Ba,' then, as I thought she would. Ba said, 'Can my new friend come with us?' I love it when a plan comes together!

Nicola said, 'I don't mind, if Grandad doesn't?' I made a grunting sound, then said, 'I suppose I'm paying again?' We laughed, while I winked at Ba's new friend!

We had a nice meal and Nicola asked all the customary questions, showing an interest in Rebekah's new friend. As we were getting ready to leave, Nicola asked her, 'Do you have any plans for this evening? Do you want to come with us up to the bar for a night's craic?'

She looked at me and I winked again. Smiling, she said, 'Yes, I would love to.'

As I went up to pay the bill, she slid up beside me, whispering, 'How did you know that would happen?'

'Because I know my daughter's heart!'

We arranged for me to collect her in an hour. Now what no-one knew was she was actually living with me, so I left Nicola up to my sister's first, with Ba, then arranged to meet them at the bar at seven or thereabouts. We rushed down home and got showered, etc. then headed up to the bar.

She asked me, 'Are you going to tell them about us this weekend?'

I said, 'Let's play it by ear,' although my thoughts were not to. 'Let's just wait till we get to Ireland next month and they are on home turf – plus, I want to have a bit of fun anyway, lol!'

We all arrived at roughly the same time. My sons had arrived by then – Lee, Curtis and Thomas. I introduced her to all and I could see my boys were impressed by her – sure why wouldn't they be? She was hot!

She was quite impressed by the different tattoos my boys had. She commented on one in particular that the boys had, which is the same on each of their arms. I told her not to mention it in front of Nicola, because it hurts her to think that they all got the same tattoo that says, 'Brothers forever', but never included her in the tatt. They insist that the rose in the centre of the tattoo is for her, but Nicola is no-one's fool and is having none of it, so we find it easier not to draw attention to it! Sisters?

As the night went on a lot of drink was consumed, although not by me, as I was designated driver. After an amazing night's craic, plus loads of singing, led by the 'Two Pats', the night came to an end. When it was time for Rebekah to go to bed the poor child was fighting sleep because of the fun she was having. Nicola and her were staying at my sister's, who happened to live just a couple of doors away.

When they were leaving, Nicola asked about how the boys, etc, were all getting home? I told her I would be making sure everyone got home, 'OK?'

My sons were staying with me at my house. As we were leaving the boys commented on how attractive they thought she was. 'Is she single?'

While she was at the toilet I said to them, 'Well, actually, she does have her eye on a member of this family.'

It was a joy to watch and listen to each one of them, 'Is it me?' 'I bet it's me.'

It sounds crazy but it warmed my heart to hear that kind of endorsement, plus it did amuse me! As we all got into the car everyone was giddy, partly through alcohol, also partly because they were all half expecting a date, ha-ha!

When we got back to my house I asked her to come in for a coffee – supposedly! I know my boys, so as they headed to bed they each gave her a hug and voiced how they hoped they would get to see her the next day for lunch, plus thanks for a great night? Once they all went to bed we had some alone time! Then I gave her a lift to her friend's, where she was staying the night!

The next day we all meet up at *The Café Plaza*, where she cooked us all brunch. I mentioned how impressed with her I was, being in work on time, considering the amount of Bacardi she drank last night! We all spent a couple of hours together with not as much conversation as the previous night – obviously they were hung over! Before they all left to head home each one of my boys quizzed me, 'Which one of us is it she fancies?'

I laughed out loud. 'You will know very soon,' I announced!

When I saw my daughter and Rebekah they were really sad to say goodbye – not only to me, but to Ba's new special friend. As I hugged my daughter she whispered, 'Dad she is a lovely person – you know, I bet if she was ten years older she would be your type.'

I gave a little laugh, 'Bit of a strange thing to say?'

She nodded, 'I know, but there's just something about her!' With that she got onto the train to head off back to Northern Ireland. I wiped my brow, 'Phew, thank goodness they never caught on!' We laughed and hugged as we headed for the car.

As we headed back home we were enjoying reliving the weekend events. She enthused about how much fun my family were and how lovely Rebekah was. As I pulled into the drive I said to her, 'When you go in, put the kettle on. I will bring the stuff I have in the boot.'

I was just about to close the boot lid when she came running out of the house, white faced and stuttering, 'We, we, we've been robbed!'

'What?' I shouted. I ran into the house, not believing her. When I got to the living room it was nearly empty of everything, except my office desk. We went into the kitchen – again almost empty! As I stopped to take it all in I noticed the hall door was closed. I said to her, with a  smile on my face, 'Open that door.'

On doing so she said, 'They must have been using the back door, because they have dropped stuff in this back hall.'

I laughed out loud and said, 'Those bloody idiots!'

This poor girl thought I had lost the plot – I was laughing, while nodding my head, 'I knew I shouldn't have left them here on their own, the shits!' laughing.

By this stage she was genuinely getting annoyed with me. 'Why are you laughing? They've taken the TV and video, but dropped the microwave? They were even trying to take all the pots and pans, but dropped some.

I said to her, 'Go open those other doors.' As she did I just kept laughing. She was really totally confused. As I lifted the microwave, I opened the door of it and found a note from my youngest son Thomas, it read, 'Told you I would get you back.'

Laughing, I explained to her that it was repayment for something I had done on him a year or so back. I explained that I went to visit him in Manchester, where he was at University. I had given off to him about the state of his flat. I told him his mum would crack up at the mess. I explained to him about how to move things when cleaning.

After taking him out for dinner and a drink we got back to his place around eleven. When he went to bed I took everything out of the kitchen, I just randomly placed them about the hall and bathroom, I left him a note telling him he didn't need to thank me – it would be easy for him to clean it properly, now, lol.

Next morning I left about six am, while he was still in bed. After saying my goodbyes, I left smiling. About four hours later he phoned, laughing, promising me vengeance and telling me it is a dish best served cold. We both laughed. I had forgotten about it till now! Well played, Thomas.

Yes, my children have inherited my sense of humour. An incident comes to mind about Lee (main man), my eldest son, who when he was at secondary school had a bit of a shock one day! Lee was not a big fan of school so much, so that there were days that he felt he should just not bother going. But, because most days his mum dropped him off at either the school bus, or at the school gate, he had developed a system whereupon he could be marked present, but didn't actually stay the whole day!

Anyway, on this particular day I had a lunch appointment with the bank manager in a restaurant in Kilkeel. As we were sitting eating and talking I looked out the window and was somewhat surprised to see my main man walking past with his arm around a blonde girl's shoulder, a cigarette hanging out of his mouth and a bottle of beer in his other hand.

After an initial shock, I excused myself and motioned to the owner of the restaurant if I could use his back door? He of course said, 'Yes,' so I made my way to the street via the back door, knowing Lee would be walking past this way.

'Hello, Lee,' I said, as he approached, oblivious to what was going on around him. I can honestly say he was not expecting to see me. He jumped, tried to spit the cigarette out, but it stuck to his lips, threw the beer into a bin and unwrapped his arm. He couldn't speak, so I just threw him the keys of my car and said, 'Jump into the car there, son, and I can give you a lift home when I'm finished here. He went to speak, but I just held my hand up, smiled and said, 'I'll be about ten minutes.'

When I finished my lunch and got into the car all Lee said was – very sheepishly, I might add – 'Sorry dad, thank you for not embarrassing me in front of my girlfri …' he didn't finish the word, which I felt was a wise decision! Since leaving school he has achieved everything he has wanted to and has a very successful career, – plus he went on to get the exams he needed! (Kids eh? Just here to torture us, ha!)

The poor girl couldn't believe it. She'd had a somewhat sheltered upbringing and definitely was not used to the crazy antics of my lot!

It reminds me of the time I went to visit my twin brother in Bedford. Now, I am by nature known as a loud person – definitely not a shrinking violet – but my twin was always known as the kinder, quieter one, except when we are together! Gordon is smaller in height than me. He is about five foot nine – he looks more like Danny DeVito's twin – not really! He is the better of the two of us, he always has been – he is considerate, patient, loving – pain in the arse! We are two sides of the same coin. To me he is always the head, while I am happy to be the tail in this particular scenario, even though I am the older twin.

'Mr bloody perfect!' (laughing now). All my life, those who know us have insisted that he, (Gordon) is the nicer twin. While privately I totally agree, in public I never would!

Anyway, as I was saying, we had driven from Wales down to London to see a show, spend a couple of days in the city. With Bedford only being an hour away we decided to go visit him for a day or two. It turned into an unexpected treat as well, because my daughter Nicola had flown over for the weekend, so it was an extra bonus for me.

We all went out for dinner, then for a drink. There was Gordon, plus his wife, Fiona – now they have been together since they were seventeen. She is an exceptional lady, who always puts family front and centre in all she does. I couldn't have wished for a better partner for my bro. She is a star, his rock, an amazing individual.

There was Natascha (Tasha), Gordon's daughter. Now Tasha is one of my favourite persons in all the world. I genuinely have a love for that girl that is only equalled by the love that I have for my own daughter. Also there was Nicola, as well as the two of us.

It was a great evening's craic. We headed back to Gordon and Fiona's house, where we continued to enjoy ourselves, then to my surprise (if I'm honest somewhat delight) Tasha started to ask – well, more like interrogate – my companion, 'Why do you like my Uncle? Isn't he too old for you? Are you after his money? Are you serious about him?'

I was intrigued, although in my mind I thought Nicola had made the bullets, whilst Tasha was firing them. I was amused – not only was she answering each and every question, she was doing so calmly with a matter of fact attitude. What clinched it for me was their last question – not sure it was meant to be her last question, but the answer kind of finished the questions! Question? 'Seriously, what do you really see in him?'

Answer … 'To be honest everything! He is all I want in a man,' (breathe). 'I love him.' Now she had told me that many times in private, but on this occasion?

Wow! With one statement she changed the whole atmosphere in the room in an instant – even my daughter smiled, acknowledging she was now willing to accept this whole relationship. Everyone was smiling as more drink was poured. I just winked at my brother – we both knew exactly what I was thinking!

Good times indeed.

It was at round about this time that a man who was a member of the church approached me for a conversation about my business – his name was Alphonso. He was similar in build to me, apart from the fact he was about six inches smaller in height. He was about forty five. He enthused about how impressed he was with my restaurant.

He went on to tell me how he and his mother had some-thing similar to it in Leicester City. He went on to explain how he had just sold it, because his wife had been offered a position in the university locally. Over the next couple of weeks he came in for coffee once or twice, when out of the blue he asked if I would consider selling?

Now I wasn't expecting that, nor did I anticipate the question. I had only owned it about eighteen months, so I hadn't thought about selling. I told him that, but did say, 'Let me think about it.' One thing I have learned over the years is never shut a door till you have a look at what's behind it.

He told me he had to go back to Leicester to finalise and tie up the loose ends with his other business there. It would be a couple of weeks before he would be back, so he asked if I would have a think? He would do the same. I thanked him, shook his hand and we parted, with me saying, 'Great, I certainly will, so give me a shout when you get back.'

# Chapter 8 – The Party

On the day of the party for my son Lee's birthday, my son Curtis had arranged to pick myself and my plus one up from the airport at one pm – which meant we would have a couple of hours to kill before the party and we had to keep out of sight.

As we came out of the airport, Curtis was waiting and when he saw me he smiled. He was happy to see me, as I was him. We embraced and then as he opened the boot he realised who I was with and, even though he behaved impeccably, once she was in the car he looked at me, laughing, 'Oh aye, "she fancies one of the family?" Now we know which one!' He winked and laughed.

Curtis is my middle son, my third child. He is a unique person with a taste for fashion, always did have. He has a bit of my personality. He looks very much like his mum's side of the family, but he definitely is an individual and free thinker. He, like his younger brother, have always followed my love of football, and Manchester United in particular, but he is a bloody nightmare to watch a match on TV with! He shouts and rants at the screen so much one can't enjoy the game. His wife laughs, but now he has his daughter joining in, so she is not laughing anymore – but we are! Lee is not into football, he is a Formula 1 man – he loves anything to do with cars!

As we were driving down towards Downpatrick, Curtis said he was lending us his car. We were booked into the hotel where the party was for bed and breakfast and he would leave us back to the airport for ten thirty am in the morning.

'Great,' I said.

We dropped him off close to my daughter's, then went to the hotel to check in – then, after we freshened up, I told her I was taking her to my spiritual chef home. We drove to Newcastle and as we turned into the drive of the famous *Slieve Donard Hotel*, I could see she was as impressed with the building as I was.

'Wow!' she said, 'you were Head Chef here?'

'I was,' I said.

'This is amazing looking – and so big. Now I understand why you are so arrogant in your whites and how you have such an understanding of hospitality.'

'What?' I said.

She laughed, 'I'm just acknowledging why you seem so arrogant at times,' she smiled. 'You know what I mean?'

I responded with, 'You mean why I'm so good?' – more a statement than question. We just smiled.

I parked and we walked up the drive, letting her take it all in. I pointed out the different entrances to the hotel, showed her the door I used for nearly ten years of my life, the back door into the kitchens. I showed here where the Elysium was – the spa – even the helicopter pad, then we walked back round to the front of the hotel and headed towards the front door of this impressive place.

As we headed in, the Concierge, whose name badge said, 'John', shook my hand firmly and welcomed us to *The Slieve Donard* – like we were royalty! She was definitely impressed.

As we went into the sumptuous foyer, with its stunning marble floor, with a red carpet leading to the reception area, we just stopped for a second to take it all in. To the left was the opulent dining room, the *Charlie Chaplin Bar* – plus, that door at the bottom takes you into the kitchen and wash up area. In front of you is Reception, on the left are the lifts, to your right a large fireplace with a false-looking fire. Straight ahead are the stairs leading to some bedrooms, as well as conference rooms – one of them being the *John Toner Room*, a former manager, whom I worked under for a time and who was a nightmare to work for, but who is now someone I call a friend.

He was an exceptional manager, who on the one hand helped my career reach great heights, but then brought me back to earth with a bang. We laugh about it now, but at the time I was not impressed at all.

What had happened was I was the second chef when the Head Chef quit unexpectedly – which means he was either sacked, or walked out without giving notice. Anyway, Mr Toner, who was the manager at the time, came and had a chat with me and suggested I fill the vacancy that had just opened up, because he felt it would be a great string in my bow and he had a great belief that I could do it.

Now even though I believed every word he said, plus I agreed with him, I felt I might be just too young, and sometimes managers say what you want to hear – in other words they talk crap! – but he convinced me it would be a good move for me and we could make it a temporary position for a month or two to see how I got on!

I thought 'OK,' so I accepted the position on a temporary basis. It was the middle of September when this happened, which was quite a busy time for us in the hotel. I promoted Joe to Second Chef and we got on with the job.

In mid-October the press did a promotional story on the hotel in time for the Christmas festivities and to encourage bookings. In that exposé they did a piece on myself, pointing out the fact I was young to be the Head Chef, but how management thought I was doing a good job.

Fast forward three weeks and I was called into said managers office for a 'chat'. The boss told me Head Office were not happy with the papers highlighting my age, so they were appointing an Executive Chef to oversee a couple of the hotels catering departments – and he would be based at the *Slieve*, which in effect meant he would be running the kitchen.

As you can imagine I was not at all happy with this news, but Mr T. convinced me it would probably only be for a week or two until the guy got settled. He started on the first of December. Unfortunately, the chef they brought in was from across the water and just didn't understand our accent or humour, but we did laugh a lot at him – I mean *with* him!

By the time Christmas was over I knew the writing was on the wall for me, because I didn't get on well with the chef at all. I went to see Mr Toner and told him I was considering leaving. This is where he could have just said, 'Goodbye,' but, fair play to him, he said, 'Give me a couple of hours to sort something.'

I did and two hours later I was offered the Head Chef's job in *Ballygally Castle Hotel* – where I actually stayed for nearly four years. I loved it there. I actually met the girl who was to become my wife and mother to my children, there, so for that I thank J.D. Toner MBE.

I remember, in 1975 when he was a young manager in the *Slieve* the then kitchen staff had a questionable sense of humour and were continually coming up with pranks to keep everyone amused. Well, on one occasion – it was the 11th of July, the day before the 'Twelfth' – someone had the idea of putting a flag on top of the hotel!

Now, you might think, 'so what?' But bearing in mind the hotel is owned by a family who are of the Protestant persuasion, to put an Irish Tricolour flag up – which represents the Catholic persuasion – is maybe a joke too far, but that's exactly what was done. On the 11th night someone placed, right at the top of the hotel, a tricolour 'fleg!'

What made it even funnier was that not one person noticed – neither the manager, nor any member of staff and, because of the timing, no one involved spoke about it openly, although we did laugh to ourselves. That was, until about 11 am, when an exasperated manager and owner came into the kitchen – and boy were they perplexed. 'Who is responsible for it?' they demanded to know.

Of course, no one acknowledged they even knew what he was talking about and the best about it was I was immediately not even regarded as a suspect, because I was a Prod! We did laugh! After all these years they still have not discovered who was responsible for it! I wonder if they ever will?

As I have said we are now firm friends. Also, I would come back to the *Slieve* a number of years later as the Head Chef – a position I would hold for six years!

She was taking it all in and I let her. I knew how captivating this place was, but I had another surprise for her. I motioned her towards the history room, where all the stories of how this place came to be, about the changes that have been made over the years. I told her to just enjoy it while I used the facilities. I said to her to look at the menus from the different periods.

When I came back I led her towards the back wall where there was a video panel, which offered a choice of up to four videos, plus earphones to listen. I gave her earphones to wear, then I pressed number 3 video. As it came to life her eyes got wider, her mouth opened – she couldn't believe she was watching and listening to me in conversation with the aforementioned John Toner MBE, plus Dermot Hughes, another former Head Chef of the hotel.

I laughed as she whispered in my ear, 'I'm so turned on by all this right now. Can we get a room?'

Fortunately, I had already got a room key – to show her the rooms (laughing)! She would definitely remember her visit to the famous *Slieve Donard.* 'Shine on you crazy diamond!'

As we got back to the hotel where we were staying we were cutting it fine for time. Thank goodness there would be food served at the party, because we were starving – we had worked up an appetite!

The party started at seven. Everyone was there, but only my kids – apart from Lee – knew I was there. By now Curtis has told them who my plus one was and they had already texted me with, 'I knew it', along with similar comments – Nicola adding that Rebekah had said it all along!

But the focus was now on Lee and his surprise party. Lee's girlfriend – who is also called Nicola – was bringing him to the hotel, supposedly just for dinner on his birthday. When he arrived, of course everyone appeared at once. He loved it. True to form, Lee took to the microphone to thank everyone for coming – he loves making speeches! He hoped they all had a great night. 'It was just a pity Dad couldn't make it,' cue laughter and applause, then enter me!

Everyone was duly impressed. As I went up on the stage to hug Lee I said into the microphone, 'You all know my first wife over there? Well, meet my next one!'

Rapturous applause, then a great night's craic ensued. Throughout the night everyone was asking when was I coming back home – to Northern Ireland – to live?

My children were starting to settle down and I was happy within myself. I had started to give thought to my future. Alphonso came into my head – I mused to give it some attention – just to see?

As we headed back to Wales we were both upbeat and sad – sad at having to leave the family, but also looking forward to the future with each other. I continually thanked God for bringing her into my life!

# Chapter 9 – Decisions

When we got back to Wales we started discussing the future. I told her about the kids wanting me to move back to Ireland. I asked her thoughts on everything?

Once again this amazing woman cut through the nonsense – she spoke straight to my heart when she said, 'My future is with you, wherever that is.'

I just lifted my head towards the sky and mouthed, 'Thank you, Lord,' and I meant it.

By this stage we had been living together for about ten months. We never really announced our relationship as a public statement, but generally people who saw us together never made any negative comment – at least not to our faces. In fact, a number of times people who did see us together used to comment that, 'You two should be a couple, you look good together!' We would just smile politely, or I would crack a joke about trying to get her to say, 'Yes'.

What I didn't know was the conversations that were happening behind closed doors. Apparently, a number of church people had opinions on everything I was doing? I was later to hear that her Mother wasn't as big a fan of mine as she professed to be! I am someone who realises that, as much as it pains me, I'm not everyone's cup of tea? (I know, I can't believe it either!)

It was around this time that Alphonso had come back from sorting out his business in Leicester. He called in to have a chat. I scheduled a meeting with him for the Friday evening after all the staff had gone home.

Alphonso was of Mexican descent, although he didn't have a very strong accent. I imagine it's an accent women would like. He was about five foot five tall, heavyset and I always felt he was a nervous man, always trying to finish the conversation quickly. I said this to him once and did ask was he in a hurry to be somewhere? But he said he was just conscious of his accent and when he came to live in UK his mum had always insisted he speak quickly! Go figure?

We discussed the business at length. I told him about the staff, the turnover, etc. I answered all his queries and after about an hour and half he said, 'OK, how much do you want for it? And please you can call me, Al?'

I replied, 'Listen, I'm happy for you to take the books away for a couple of days, have your accountant go over them. Let's meet back here next Friday, same time, and if you're still interested then we can talk money, or you make me an offer?'

We shook hands and parted company. When I got home I told her about what we had discussed. She asked why didn't I give him a price? I explained that I wanted him to feel that I was open to his accountant putting a valuation on the business, because had I told him what I wanted then he would have come back and said 'Oh, my accountant says its only worth this.'

'But I have now reversed it, so when he comes back to me, whatever price he says I know it should be an honest valuation, then we can make a decision on what happens next.'

Over the next week I started entertaining the idea of moving back to Northern Ireland. We both discussed our options. She asked if I would buy a business when, or if, we go back?

'I don't know,' was the honest answer. 'Let's see what happens when Al comes back to me – then we will have all the information? But for now we have to concentrate on the next gourmet night in a fortnight, as well as deciding what is going to happen come Christmas time, as its only eight weeks away. Are we going to have a gourmet dinner night, or try to get a couple of Christmas Party nights booked, instead?' We decided on the latter and started to advertise as such!

Al came as planned, we sat down to talk, and I asked him what his accountant thought of everything? He indicated his accountant had said it seemed like a good business, plus his valuation was at what I thought was not too far off my own valuation.

I didn't immediately say anything, I was just letting it sink in, when he added, 'Obviously, you will feel he has undervalued it, so I am willing to add another couple of thousand pounds to that and that's my offer. What do you think?' he said.

In truth, I was a bit surprised, because what he offered was about one thousand more that I would have settled for. I said, 'Give me twenty four hours to mull it over. I will let you know.'

'Why?' he said, quite anxiously.

I replied, 'I just need to run it by my accountant to hear his thoughts.' I tried to reassure him that it was all OK.

'No one else is talking to you about buying it, are they?'

I was surprised by this question and I really should have been more aware of his whole demeanour, but hindsight is a wonderful education. All I see is my plans coming together and my head is totally ruling my heart, or is it the other way round?

Twenty four hours later after speaking to Ron, and naturally my other half, I decided to accept Al's offer. If I am honest, I had decided to accept it the minute he made it, but prudence made me wait. He was overjoyed. I put his obvious over excitement down to his Mexican blood, but he just seemed – I don't know – a bit too over the top!

He said, 'OK, I can take over from Monday next week?'

I said, 'Whoa, it's not going to happen that fast. It's now November and it will take about six weeks to sort out all the legal stuff, so I suggest you leave or bring a deposit either into me, or through the solicitor – that will start the ball rolling.'

'What you think? I will give you two thousand pounds, now,' he says, 'then you tell me when I can take over?'

'I love your enthusiasm, Al, but relax. I will ask my solicitor to draw up a contract. You sort out the deposit on Monday, or Tuesday? Then I think realistically it will be about six or seven weeks to finalise everything, OK? In the meantime, we keep it between us and our solicitors.'

We shook hands. I do know how stupid it sounds, but his keenness to get in, without the legal side of it being sorted, unnerved me a bit, if I'm being totally honest.

Al phoned me Monday at about nine thirty. I laughed and told him, 'I only just spoke to my solicitor – goodness, you're keen! Listen, I should have the pre-contract paper here by five pm, so call about seven this evening. We can sort it then and I will have an idea about how quickly it can be sorted.'

At bang on seven he appeared. I offered him a coffee, which he accepted. He drank double espressos – I don't know how anyone can drink double strength espresso! Ugh, I hate coffee! Anyway, as we sat down I showed him the pre-contract which he just glanced over, then went to sign. I gestured as if to move the page, I said to him, 'Al, are you sure you're happy with this and what it says?'

'Yes, yes,' he said, 'I am happy. When can I move in?'

I thought to myself, maybe he can't read too good, so I gently told him what it said, 'Now it just says you're paying a deposit of  …?? How much of a deposit do you want to pay?'

He pulled a load of twenties out of his pocket and said, 'Three thousand pounds.'

I was genuinely surprised at this, 'Don't you want to do it by cheque or Bankers Draft?'

'No,' he said, 'cash is king!'

'Well,' I said, 'OK, you understand because all the legal papers, etc. are going to take about six weeks it will be about Christmas week before you can take over?'

'OK,' he says, then he asked, 'Are you closed for Christmas?'

I said, 'Good point, we are actually – from Christmas Eve for a week. I know,' I said, 'let's make it that you take over on December twenty eighth. That is when we would normally be back to work in preparation for opening again after the holidays?'

'OK,' he said, 'If I have to wait till then, fine, but can we not open until the thirtieth so we will have two days to do the handover?'

I nodded, 'Fine.'

He asked if I wanted him to count the money out on the table? Goodness, I had forgotten the cash.

I laughed, 'No, that's fine,' I said, 'I will trust you and thank you!'

For the second time a red light came on in my head, but again I dismissed it. I mean, seriously, a man is buying a business, but doesn't mind just handing over cash, without any kind of receipt, or acknowledgement? Still, I have three thousand pounds in my pocket and a definite plan for moving forward. I think to myself Christmas will definitely be good for us!

# Chapter 10 – End of an Era

We started to concentrate on the Christmas period that would be coming up very soon. We set about preparing menus, plus everything else that was needed to make this festive season our best one yet, because this could be our last one in this place and I wanted it to be spectacular!

It was the beginning of December and every-thing was moving in the right direction, when out of the blue I got a phone call from an old buddy of mine, Mark. He was calling to suss me out? He was looking for some-one like me – his words – to work with him in setting up a new restaurant complex in Northampton direction.

I asked him for all the details? He explained that he was the number two. It was for a new caravan park complex, opening in about six or seven months in that part of the world, and he needed someone to help design the kitchen, layout of the restaurant, café, function room, etc. 'I need someone like yourself, Grey – one thing I notice about the English and Welsh is they abbreviate names – who knows how to price stuff, make sure its ordered and all, plus get it in situ when it gets here? You know anybody?'

'When do you need them?' I asked.

'Four, maybe five, months, or thereabouts? Plus, I can give them a van to use.'

'A van?' I asked.

'Caravan, you numpty!' he laughed.

'Wow, thank you, Lord,' I thought to myself, 'Actually, Mark,' I quipped, 'your timing couldn't be better!'

I told him that I myself could be available at the right price. I explained my situation to him, which he was happy to hear, so we negotiated a price and I agreed to do a six month contract, starting third January. We arranged to meet at a lodge in the lake district on twenty seventh of December for a night's craic. The best bit was the lodge was owned by the company we would be working for, so it was free! Absolutely marvellous!

As Christmas was almost upon us our focus changed more quickly to sorting it out. While all this was going on, I was continually checking with my solicitor about the business transfer and also giving my notice to my house landlord, who seemed genuinely sad to see me go.

I informed my close friends at the church of my decision to move on, and had arranged to have an evening's craic at my home before Christmas to say farewell. This was when we first really found out that, although I had made a lot of good friends over the last number of years, I – or we – discovered a lot of the persons we had invited suddenly couldn't make it.

At first I didn't think anything of it, until one of my friends from the prayer group hinted to me that he felt it wouldn't be as big a crowd as I thought?

'Huh?' I said, 'what am I missing here?

He said, 'Oh? You do know her Mum is stirring the pot, because you're 'taking her daughter away' and she doesn't believe that her daughter really wants to go, plus implying other not so nice stuff?'

It's not very often I get angry, but this pissed me off – so much so that they had originally been invited to the party, but I really can't stand two-faced people, so I suggested to my other half to have a word with her mum and explain to her that I did not groom her daughter and that she had a mind of her own!

Even though there were only about thirty at the party (not her mum), we had an amazing night's craic! I would really miss this group of people.

Everyone was also sad to see me leaving the restaurant and couldn't believe I was selling it – speaking of which, Alphonso was invited to the shindig, but couldn't make it, but the Vicar – with whom I had a conversation about

Alphonso, which only heightened my already niggling thoughts about the man – was there, but I again pushed them out of my mind.

Christmas came and we had the best year's trading since I came to Aber, which made for a great holiday period! We were looking forward to new horizons, to bigger and better things!

We had almost everything sorted with work, the house, plus the staff had been told. I had given them all a nice Christmas bonus, because they had helped me achieve the success we were having and I always pay it forward. They all seemed happy – especially Coreen, who told me she was just a hundred pounds short for her boob job.

I laughed and said, 'Tell you what, if you let me see them when you get them done you can have the hundred.' and she said, 'Yes.' so I handed it over, knowing that I would never see her or them, laughing. She actually sent me a picture of them through *Facebook* about six months later – money well spent, I think, lol!

A couple of days later we were heading to the Lake District for our night of craic with Mark. When we arrived we took it in turn to introduce our partners – I introduced my girlfriend to Mark, then he introduced his girlfriend, Maureen, to us. What was really interesting was his girlfriend was the same age as my girlfriend and he was nearly the same age as me!

We had a spectacular evening and the food was exquisite. Real friendships were forged that evening, which are still strong today.

Mark also told me how delighted he was that I would be joining him in January and he was looking forward to us working together again, because he knew the craic would be great.

'Just one thing,' he said, 'my boss, who is also your boss, hates Manchester United with a passion, so I didn't tell him you support them. So don't tell him, right?'

I laughed, 'He must be a Leeds fan then?'

'That he is!' said Mark.

'I do love a challenge!' I laugh.

As we headed back to Aber the next morning, we reflected on the previous night. We started discussing how things seemed to be coming together for us. It all just seemed perfect!

We were supposed to have everything finalised with Al on the day before *The Café Plaza* was due to open again. *The Plaza* was closed until the thirtieth, which was going to give me a couple of days to help familiarise him with everything.

On the thirtieth we had arranged to meet at noon to sign everything and finalise payment, etc. He changed it to the next day. I was just sitting relaxing as he came through the door. I got up and shook his hand. I thought his hand was very sweaty, but before I could speak he was apologising, while taking money out of his pocket?

'No,' I thought, 'is he going to pay me all this money in cash?'

No he wasn't!

'Listen,' he said, 'I have a slight problem. My mother didn't sign the release at the bank. She is away for Christmas and won't be back till early January?'

I could hear my words repeating in my head, 'It's all coming together perfectly.' I couldn't believe what I was hearing! This was the man who had been badgering me to get in as soon as possible to take over, who had phoned me every week and tortured me. I had everything else sorted to move.

'Damn? Don't panic Graham, he's not getting his money back! Shit, what I am going to do? Think!'

'OK', I said, 'so what are your thoughts now?'

'Well,' he said, 'I am going to give you another fifteen hundred pounds now, as a show of good faith, but you have my assurance that you will have the rest by bank transfer by tenth January.'

'Wow, I am supposed to hand over my business to you today, trusting that you will be honourable?'

'Yes,' he said, 'listen, you can phone my solicitor, who will confirm this!'

I was at a loss to know what to do. Every part of me was screaming, 'NO! NO! NO!' but in my heart I had moved on and wanted to get out. My mind was working at twenty to the dozen. 'OK,' I said, 'if your legal representative confirms your story I will go ahead. We can complete the paperwork. I will trust you. I'll take the money you're offering today, but I will be honest here, Al, when I say I will be very disappointed – and I don't like being disappointed! I knew it was a weak attempt at sounding menacing, but what else could I do ?

After speaking with his solicitor I was inclined to accept what was said, so I agreed to let him deal with my solicitor to sort it and he gave me another fifteen hundred pounds that he had on him. I gave him all the keys and necessary codes for the alarm, etc. – plus all the staff details. I showed him how the cookers and equipment in the kitchen worked. I honestly didn't believe he heard or listened to half of what I was saying, he was that excited, but, hey, we have all been there – 'each to their own.' I shook his hand firmly, wishing him every success and I meant it!

I set about saying goodbye to the favourite people I had met and formed real friendships with. I allowed a bit of extra time to say goodbye to Heather, my first Assistant Cook when I arrived here all those years ago. Heather was special.

She was a looker. My pet name for her was, Butterfly – she just seemed to float and was always on the go. She was about five foot two, with long blonde hair. I think she was what is considered a real Welsh lass. She spoke Welsh fluently and made it sound sexy – Bow Wow! She was married, a real homemaker. She had two children – a girl, called Cerri, plus a lad, called Dean.

Now Dean was an exceptional boy, I loved that kid, I still do. He worked part time with me in the kitchen, and reminded me of my own boys. He could be a cheeky shit, but he had a heart the size of a lion.

I remember one of the times I was going to Manchester to watch United play, I asked did he want to come with me? He jumped at the chance. I said, 'OK, if your mum allows it I will take you'. She, of course, said, 'Yes.' He was excited as we headed off to Manchester. En route we picked up my nephew and, of course, my beloved. I had also arranged to meet Thomas, my youngest son, outside the ground.

Anyway, the craic was good traveling up to the match and when we got there and parked up I messaged Thomas to tell him where I was standing. Next thing he jumps me from behind, nearly gives me a bloody heart attack! As I turned round I realised Curtis, plus his mate, David, were also there. I was delighted to see them all.

We had a great evening's craic, plus United won to cap it all. I took them all for a pizza afterwards and there was much merriment, plus they teased not only Dean, but my other half, about how the house had been a mess and they couldn't believe how the burglar left all the stuff in the hall!

As we headed back to the car I asked Curtis when he was heading back home? He said, 'Friday, or Saturday, – depends if Thomas can get mum to cough up for a flight home for him at the weekend?'

'Ha-i-yelp!' I'd been conned again?

'That's what this is all about, you pulling all the stops out to fleece me? I bloody knew it', I laughed.

'Hey,' Thomas suggested, 'why don't we all go back with you to Aber till Friday, Dad? It will be a bit of craic?'

'Great idea,' Curtis agreed. David thought so, too – not that he had any choice, as he was staying with Curtis, lol!

'Wait a minute, Dean said, 'Where is everyone going to sit in the car?'

They all laughed and said, 'You're in the boot, mate!'

When we got back to the car and as we all climbed in, because Dean was the smallest, he ended up sitting in the front well of the car on his honkers between my girlfriends legs, who thankfully was wearing jeans. Aw, Dean we did laugh that night! Love you Deano!

It was later that night she told me that she was jealous of the relationship I had with my family and that she was genuinely surprised how nice they were. I did tell her that most of the credit should go to their mother, who was and is an exceptional human being!

# Chapter 11 – New Bed

We took the decision that I would travel up to the new place on my own, initially, so she stayed behind at her parents' house. We thought it would be for a week, or two, to allow me time to get settled.

I arrived late afternoon Saturday. Mark had arranged for the keys of my new place to be left at the security gate – along with a map to find it! I found it after a couple of detours, lol! I unpacked, then checked the place out.

As I wasn't starting until Monday, I decided to drive over to Bedford, which is only twenty minutes away, to visit my brother – who was delighted to see me. We had an evening meal, as well as a few drinks, and he suggested I stay the night. I phoned my beloved. I said to her, 'I don't know if I can survive two weeks without you?' We both laughed, because tonight was to be the first night we had not shared a bed in over two years!

The next morning I awakened after a restless sleep. The first thing I did was phone her and ask how she slept? She moaned she didn't sleep well. 'Me neither,' I said, 'so I think you should just get the train down here today, then I will pick you up at station, how does that sound?'

'Yippee!' she shouted, 'I have already packed.'

I just know she is telling the truth, 'Ha, great!' I say. 'Let me know what time the train gets in and I will be waiting!'

'Absolutely brilliant,' I think to myself. 'When it's right you just know it's the right thing to do!'

I met her off the train with a yellow ribbon wrapped around me, but she hadn't a clue what I was meaning. I laughed and sang the song 'Oh, tie a yellow ribbon …' Nothing! ha-ha. It was wasted on her – the youth of today! Anyway, we were both ecstatic to be together again. You would have sworn we had been apart for months, instead of one night. Love? 'That's amoré!'

Monday morning I headed over to the office as arranged and met Mark, who introduced me to everyone, 'Hi, G,' he said, 'this is Simon the main man.'

We shook hands and I instantly took a liking to him. He was about six foot four, broad shoulders and a great Yorkshire accent, which made me say to him, 'With an accent like that you must be a Leeds supporter?'

I kept talking, telling him that my Mum was a Leeds fan all her life. He gave a big broad smile and said, 'Obviously a woman of wisdom. Is your Mum still with us?' he asked.

'Sadly not,' I said, 'and even though we tried to get her to see sense, she passed away still loving Leeds!' He stood up and said forcefully, 'Please don't tell me you are a bloody scum United fan?'

I winked at him and said, 'You just can't get away from us!'

We both laughed and he quipped, 'I like this guy!'

Then I was introduced to Vinny, who was the bar manager – a smaller man, 'He's quite young,' I thought. I was right, he was twenty four. This was his first management role, but he seemed confident enough. I was introduced to Mary, the housekeeper, plus Terry, who was the maintenance officer.

Introductions over Simon set out the road map for opening the new site and its amenities. 'We have between three and six months to get it all sorted,' he said, 'Each person here is responsible for their own department. As long as you keep within your budget you have almost total control over your employees – remembering they will probably need security checked, so give the relevant forms to Felicity in the office, who will sort that out.'

After about two hours of listening and some minor discussions, Simon finished with, 'OK, we will all meet every Thursday at eleven am for an update from each department on all aspects of their department. Any questions?

No? Great! Each head of department go to the office, where you will sign for your keys, understanding this, DO NOT LOSE THEM, OR LEND THEM TO ANYBODY!'

'Plus, get all the necessary paperwork, etc. You will need that for copies of all your budget, costings, suppliers and the like. Any queries, or questions, your first port of call is Mark. If he can't answer, or doesn't know them, then come see me.'

After a round of applause and a, 'Good luck, folks!' we all went to start our new jobs properly!

My first new recruit was, as you would expect, my own amazing assistant cook – who was obviously over-joyed to be working alongside me again. I then set about doing the job I was paid to do. I was even able to give one of my friends from back home a turn. He ran *The Chef Shop* in Belfast, which supplied catering equipment to our industry. I always liked to give him an order – after all 'a constant drip fills the bucket!'

We did enjoy those first couple of months in that park and laughed a lot. The work was hard some days, but we had some great fun – like the time Simon came into the kitchen with Mark and said to me, 'Hi, Irish' – he called me that – 'my wife is coming down next week and I want you to do a special meal for her, if that's OK?'

'Not a problem,' I said, 'What day?'

'Next Thursday,' he said – I gave him a thumbs up.

'Has she any allergies, or is she a veggie?'

'No,' he laughed, 'she's married to me, so she is obviously normal!'

I laughed and said, 'You probably believe that, too.'

Mark joined in with laughing, then Simon said, 'Actually, I'm just thinking, do either of you two know any good pranks I could play on her when she is here?'

Mark said, 'He's your man,' pointing at me. 'He knows some great ones.'

I asked Simon, 'What have you told your wife about me?'

'Nothing much, just that you're a scum United supporter, you're Irish, plus you've got a young bird.'

I laughed, 'Right, over the next couple of days drop into the conversation when you're talking to her that your Chef – who is actually British! – has Tourette's and it takes a bit of getting used to. Plus, his girlfriend – not 'bird'! – is younger than him.'

'Sounds a cracking idea!' we all started laughing like little schoolboys.

'Also,' I said as an afterthought, 'tell Daisy (his daughter) to tell her as well, but make sure it's in a matter of fact way!'

'OK,' he said.

Now, while all this was going on I was still having to deal with the fact that we still hadn't completed the sale of *The Cafe Plaza!* Al's mother was still not back – apparently! Aggh!

He did a further bank transfer for another two thousand pounds into my account. I tried phoning him on more than one occasion, to find out what was happening, but I was finding it hard to contact him! My solicitor wasn't much better. I felt myself getting more and more frustrated.

I decided to write to him directly – which I did – and I explained how annoying and frustrating this was getting and how I wasn't selling him a business through a Hire Purchase agreement – and that whilst it was great him sending me money every couple of weeks I was now at the stage where I had to give him a definitive deadline to complete, or I would have no option other than to cancel the sale – whereupon we would both lose money, with him losing monies he had already paid!

Four days later he phoned me, full of apologies – obviously remorseful. He started trying to explain, telling me all about his problems, but I cut him short saying,

'Al, forgive me, but you have until the 20th February to get it signed, with all balance to be paid, or I will have no option but to cancel the sale – which means you will lose your deposit! End of!'

I hung up the phone, rang my solicitor and told him what had just transpired.

He said, 'OK, I will send him a letter to that effect, just to keep it all legal!'

I came off the phone with a feeling in my gut that this wasn't going to go as I had planned!

We decided we would go out for dinner that evening and we went to a local bar/restaurant just up the road. As we were sitting down in walked Mark with his woman.

'Great minds,' I said. He smiled. I beckoned them to come join us. The girls hugged like they were besties. We had a nice evening, talking about nothing – really just enjoying each other's company. As we were getting ready to leave Mark asked, 'How do you like living on the park?'

She and I looked at each other and smiled. I said, 'It's like living in a block of flats, all on ground level. Ha! Any particular reason for the question?'

'Well, actually, yes. About another mile or so up the road there's another smaller park that our crowd own and you might see something there you like?'

'Well, I know where we are going now!' I said.

When we left we headed for the other park. Mark was right, it was only about a mile up the road. First impression was very good – it was down a private road, lined with trees either side, and as you got to the bottom there were little parks, holding only two or three mobile homes in each park.

We pulled into a car parking space in front of what looked like a shop. As we exited the car a man in his late sixties, I guess, came out of said shop with a beaming smile. 'Good evening.' he said, in a thick Yorkshire accent.

I looked at him more closely and took a stab in the dark? 'Simon's Father?' I said.

'Indeed!' he said, 'how can you tell?'

'Goodness, looks like you just spat him out.' I said, laughing. 'He is almost your double!'

'And you must be the famous chef I've heard about, with the Irish accent?' he smiled, hand outstretched, which I took.

'Northern Irish,' I said, smiling. I introduced him to my company.

'The pleasure is all mine,' he said, with a twinkle in his eye. Lol, I definitely like Yorkshire men. There is just something about them!

I told him why we had interrupted his evening. He explained that this park was mostly owner vans only, and he pointed to one sitting to the left of where we were standing.

He said, 'This one is a three bed, two bathroom one that the owner might rent out, as his job is taking him away. Unfortunately, he's actually in there now packing up. So, if you want a word, just knock the door. Normally, owners ask us to sell them for them, because we usually move them on pretty quickly – but it's January and we officially close for six weeks at this time of year – but, sure, have a chat with him.' He winked at me. 'Just remember,' he said, 'he is looking for a quick sale!'

I knocked the door. As it was opened I smiled, put my hand out to shake his. I introduced myself and asked him, 'Can we look around?'

'Of course,' he said, 'come ahead.'

As he was showing us he enquired, 'Are you looking for it as a holiday home, or more permanent?'

I explained, 'We have started work in the main park, so we are looking for an upgrade from what we are in.'

'Great!' he said, 'Well, this should suit you great. The top bedroom is ensuite, and then there is also another bathroom shower here – so your daughter could have her own shower room.'

We just smiled. I said, 'Great. How much are you looking for it?'

'Well, to tell you the truth,' he said, 'it's worth more than I'm asking, but I'm flying to Dubai with work, so I don't need the hassle!'

'How long you going for?' I asked.

'Indefinitely,' he said. 'It's promotion. I've no-one to pass it on to and I don't want to be paying the ground rent, plus all the upkeep fees, etc.'

'Price?' I interjected.'

He smiled and said it breaks his heart, but he will take two thousand seven hundred and fifty.

I thought for a minute, remembering what Simon's dad had said. I said, 'I can give you two thousand today! Plus, I'm talking cash!'

I put my hand out as if to shake on a deal. He scratched his chin. He said, 'Put another two hundred and fifty to it and you have a deal.' We shook hands.

An hour later we had a new home! 'I love it when a plan comes together!' The only downside was she might have to walk to work some days, because we wouldn't always be on the same shift, but she insisted it was not a problem. She could always run up the road. Anyway, if it was raining really badly I could come pick her up. Yay, cracker!

We moved in over the weekend and we got our own stuff delivered – our own bed, plus our sofa, etc. It didn't take long to make it into our home, plus, it gave her a chance to sew up curtains and make small crafty things – which she was great at doing!

We were two days away from Simon's wife, Michelle, arriving. I had made up an amazing menu for them for their dinner evening. I was, as was everyone else, looking forward to me pranking the poor woman. I think half the park had heard about what was going to happen, because everyone and their auntie was coming up to me hoping to talk to me about it. I told Simon we really needed to stop the chatter or someone might get offended – then I could be in hot water – but this pantomime was going to happen and I had a starring role.

Thursday came, all the scenes were set. Michelle was bringing in some paintings she had done – I love good paintings, so I was looking forward to seeing them. Daisy came running excitedly into the kitchen about two thirty, 'She's here, Chef, ha. Come on, quick.'

'Relax,' I said, 'play it normal.'

I pretended to be carrying out menu cards to the bar. As I walked out I noticed half the staff were hovering about and I looked behind me and half the kitchen staff were coming out! No pressure, ha!

Simon said, 'Hello, Chef, come meet the wife.'

As I walked towards her I noticed two things – she had really sparkly eyes and a great chest. I extended my hand towards her – just as she went to take it I made an exaggerated jerk movement and in a rather loud voice I said, 'Whoa, big tits,' couple of swear words, then finished with, 'sparkling diamonds.' Now, almost calmly, 'Hello, nice to meet you.'

I smiled. Poor woman nearly jumped a mile. As I took her hand she was still trembling, but she did her best to act normal. If she had lifted her head she would have noticed her husband and half the staff were rolling about in stitches! Anyway, I gave it a couple of minutes – commenting how nice her paintings were, then just as she started to relax, I did it again, throwing in a few swear words, while insulting her backside. Then I casually headed towards the kitchen.

Needless to say, Simon and Mark came in to reward me with an Oscar, laughing their legs off. My heart went out to Michelle. I kept it up for about two and a half hours by periodically having an 'outburst.' After that I went to her – firstly, to make sure she hadn't started taking Valium; secondly, to apologise.

As I approached her I could see the nervousness in her eyes. I smiled, then said, 'Michelle, I am sorry if I frightened you, but blame your husband.'

She said, 'Don't be silly, you have nothing to be sorry for. You can't help it.'

I laughed, 'Actually, I can. I don't have Tourette's – it was all a joke!'

She genuinely didn't believe me – which, of course, made it all the funnier, especially for the audience that had gathered, who were now applauding. She looked around and once she saw her husband she looked at me in surprise, then burst out laughing. She give me a big hug. 'You were brilliant. I believed it, totally.' But then she said, 'Who thought of this – because it definitely wasn't him?' pointing to her husband. Cue more laughter.

Some days work is brilliant! We dined out on this story many times since. Whenever we meet up, or talk, it still gets a laugh.

We were about two weeks away from Al completing in Wales. I was in touch with my solicitor on a regular basis, but still no movement – then, about eight days before completion, Al sent me a text offering to send me more money. I phoned my solicitor and he said, 'Don't accept it, or he can push back everything.'

So, believing he knew what he was talking about, I listened to him inform Al, 'No let's just complete on the twentieth.'

As with most things in my life, when one area is going great there is always something else trying to keep you down.

One day as myself, Simon and Mark were walking around the outside of the complex, to see how it was all coming together, I noticed a wee Vespa-like scooter and it had a 'For Sale' sign on it.

'Hey,' I asked, 'who is selling this?'

Simon told me it was one of the electricians and he was not asking a fortune either!

I said, 'OK, I will catch up.' and I broke off to go see David the electrician, who just happened to be coming out of building.

'David?' I shouted.

'Yes, Chef?'

I called him over to me as I waited by the scooter. 'Yes?' he said.

'Tell me about this yoke,' I said.

He told me everything I needed to know. It had just passed its MOT test and was driving great. He was upgrading to a car.

'Price?'

He told me what he wanted, but I told him, 'Dick Turpin wore a mask!'

After a bit of back and forward we agreed a price and shook hands. He was to deliver it to me at the back door when he finished his shift.

I caught up to the other two and they teased me about ripping the young fellow off. I just laughed.

Come six o'clock I summoned her to the back and made her cover her eyes as I had two surprises for her. Of course, as with everything in this place, nothing was private – so about five people headed out to see as well. When we got to the back door the scooter was in position and covered with a tarpaulin – to make it look like something else. I stood her in front of it and then took the blindfold off.

'What is it?' she asked, excited.

I said, 'Guess.'

She guessed wrong about three times, then gave up and I said, 'OK, just pull off the cover.'

As she did she started jumping up and down – I swear it was only when I gave her a surprise that I noticed the age difference! She was refreshingly honest in her happiness. It reminded me of my own kids on Christmas morning! Damn!

She was absolutely delighted with the scooter and after riding up and down the back yard she eventually relaxed. Suddenly, she said to me, 'Hey, I thought you said two surprises?'

For a split second I had thought about maybe cancelling the second one, but when I looked at her I knew I had to go through with it!

'Oh yes,' I said, 'I nearly forgot.' I winked. 'Lift the seat and look in the pocket?'

She got off the bike. After putting it on its stand, she proceeded to lift the seat. Next thing she looked up with tears in her eyes, 'Is this what I think it is?'

I nodded and said, 'Will you?' but before I could finish she was jumping into my arms, crying, shouting, 'Yes! Yes! Yes!'

It was then that the others noticed that she was putting on an engagement ring. A couple of weekends before, when we were in Bedford, we had been walking around the town and when we passed the jewellers we window shopped the rings. Then she showed me the 'one' – should

I ever want to put a ring on it! 'Double Brownie points, today, methinks.' lol!

She said to me later that night, 'You know, today was one of the best days of my life. I am so happy.'

I told her I hoped that was a sentiment I would hear again and again – plus, for the record, it had been one of mine, too! Even better, like me she didn't need a big party, she was just happy!

# Chapter 12 – New Address

While all this happiness was going on I was still getting grief from Wales – in the shape of Al. The 20th came and went, and still nothing – so I informed the solicitor to start proceedings. This was a route I really didn't want to go down, but I had no option. Boy, did I open a can of worms!

Before it even got to court I was informed that Al had closed the premises, paid off the staff and – because it wasn't trading – the landlord had taken back possession of the property. So, I would have to take a case against him as well, which was a bloody joke! I then found out Al had health issues – and not, it seemed, physical! – which meant that, whatever way it went, I was going to be out a fortune trying to sort this all out. I was also a couple of hundred miles away, so I had to make a decision?

I talked it over with Simon whose opinion I respected. He suggested cutting my losses, because it would only cost me more trying to take it legal. 'Just sell everything in the shop, get yourself that money,' – which is exactly what I tried to do, but only succeeded in selling part of the inventory, before the landlord took out an injunction against me, because there was rent owing – not by me! He was reclaiming ownership of his property.

By this stage I was sick to the back teeth with it all, so I just gave up and walked away from it – in truth I ran! To be honest, had I known all of Al's issues from the start and acted on my gut feelings I'd have handled it all completely differently! I just had to accept it as a failure and move on!

A fortnight later my solicitor sent me a bill. I laughed at him and told him straight that had he let Al give me the last money he offered I might have paid him, but as it stood, I genuinely didn't believe he had done his due diligence, etc.

Needless to say I was being told by certain people that it was my own fault and if I had been concentrating less on my girlfriend, and more on my business, it could have turned out a whole lot different! That hurt, because all she had been was supportive. I can honestly say – rightly or wrongly – I was the one who was driving this decision. People can be so fickle and opinionated! And they were my friends?

After what happened in Wales I was feeling sorry for myself – but I must say, she was really patient with me and just let me work it off by allowing me to just be me! I focused on the job in hand and we continued to develop the restaurant, etc. and the place was coming together well.

After a couple of months we started chatting about our next move. She was happy wherever we went. Mark had mentioned to me that there was a new place being opened in Scotland and he was thinking of doing it and would I be interested in going with him?

I said, 'Let me think about it for a day or two.'

I mentioned it to her and asked for her thoughts, but she thought we would be better going back to Northern Ireland – mainly because of the family – but, also, she felt it was the right time for me. I pondered what she was saying and I thought, 'Yeah, she is right.' So I told Mark my decision. It turned out he didn't go either!

As we only had about six weeks left there I rang the only sister who lives back home and told her I was thinking about coming back to N.I. Could she look for a house for me to rent, initially? She, being wonderful, said, 'Of course!'

She phoned me about a week later and told me she had found two which would suit – one was a three bedroom detached, the other one was a two bed semi. I chatted it over with her indoors and she thought the two bed would be better as it was only going to be for about six months, until we decided what we wanted to do further down the line. So, I relayed that to my sister, who set about sorting it out for us.

We could collect the keys on July fifteenth. I just needed to pay the deposit to secure it – which I duly did. So, with the house sorted, I just needed to organise  some work. I phoned a friend of mine who owned an employment agency and gave him my homecoming date.

'Leave it with me,' he said.

He called back the next day and said, 'You start on 20th July on an eight month contract.' Brilliant! Work sorted. Now, one more thing to sort. 'Where is your passport?' I asked her. 'Is it up to date?' She looked wide eyed and said, 'Do you need a passport to get into Northern Ireland? We didn't the last time!'

I laughed out loud, 'No, but you need one to get into Italy – which is where we are heading first!' I never tired of her gleeful hugs! There was a genuine quality about her that just lifted my spirit!

I headed over to the park shop and mentioned to Simon's Dad that I was leaving in about five weeks, so if he could sell my van he would be on a good percentage. He laughed. About two weeks later it was sold for three grand and after his percentage I was well satisfied.

We had to vacate the caravan a couple of days before our finish date and spent the last couple of nights back on the main park. We finished working on June 30th. There was no fanfare, or big goodbyes – just a few handshakes. My nephew, Kian, had brought a van over from Bedford for all our stuff and was going to put it in his garage for storage. 'Don't forget my scooter!' was repeated a couple of times – 'Ha, I won't,' was an exasperated response – 'Flip, she goes on a bit, doesn't she?' laughed Kian.

As Kian headed for Bedford we thanked him and wished him a safe journey. We headed for Liverpool, for the John Lennon Airport. I should point out here that this is 'real love', because I <u>hate</u> flying! We holidayed in Sorento, Italy, where we had an amazing time! I love Italy. It has to be one of the best places in the world. I have been several times. We were really looking forward to the sunshine. I love the language – it is brilliant. Forgive me if I don't talk about the flight – for me it's like a white knuckle ride at the funfair. I just hate it! I left her to talk to the lady seated next to her – I like to concentrate on my fear!

By the time we arrived at our destination it was about ten pm, so we just grabbed a drink at the bar then had an early night. Next morning the sun was splitting the trees – absolutely stunning! After breakfast we went for a walk around the town to get a look at this glorious place.

Sorrento is almost two towns in one. As we walked out of the hotel – which is situated in what appears to be the town centre – we wandered around, commenting on how everything didn't seem that old, yet if you followed the signs to the 'Old Town' – which only seemed about a mile away – you came across a long high wall. If you followed it for a short distance, then turned left it was like stepping back in time. Honestly, we were both amazed and fascinated by the sight we beheld. It was charming – so old-worldly.

'It reminds me of the 'Godfather' films,' I told her.

'Never watched them!' she said.

'What! You've never watched the Godfather?'

She shook her head. I was shocked, 'I don't believe you? Right, you're in for a treat when we get home!'

On day three of our holiday we headed to the local theatre, where we knew there was some kind of concert on – even though we didn't know who was playing. We figured it would be a night's craic. Turned out it was part of the James Last Orchestra! The man himself wasn't there, but still it was a thoroughly enjoyable evening, plus there was a big crowd, which made the atmosphere great, as well.

When the concert was over we headed back to the hotel, where there was Karaoke going on in the bar. She looked at me, smiling.

I offered, 'It would be rude not to.'

We both laughed. The good thing about holidaying in a foreign country is no one knows you, so you convince yourself you're better than you really are, lol! Plus, I do like the applause – even if it is out of pity!

On one of the last days there I played a prank on her. We had gotten to know some of the staff in the bar. It turned out one of them had a sister who was a policewoman – so we arranged for me to be arrested in the street. It was hilarious! I played my part well, but the policewoman deserved a Bafta – she was brilliant! She spoke good English and approached me, gun out, saying I looked like a jewel thief they were looking for. She made me stand against the wall and stretch them.

My girlfriend was panicking – trying to convince her we were just there on holiday. Her panic turned to annoyance when the policewoman laughed and then kissed me on both cheeks, with a 'Ciao!' I did enjoy pranking her – for some reason she didn't! Go figure? We laugh about it now!

We had an amazing couple of days sightseeing and just being tourists, but we were looking forward to heading home – although I had to go through another ordeal on that bloody plane. Ah!

When we got back from Italy we had planned to go back to Aber for a day, so she could spend time with her family before we headed to Ireland. I dropped her off at her parents' house and arranged to see her the next day, so she could have some private time with her family, and I would stay at my sister's for the night.

The next morning as I bade my sister goodbye, she cautioned me to make sure I knew what I was doing, because she had heard rumours that criticised me? I assured her I did and that I was really happy – plus, I believed this would go the distance. She wished me well and I left.

We had arranged to meet in town at a local eatery for breakfast. When she arrived she was with her mum, which didn't bother me too much. We ordered breakfast and drinks – tea for her, hot water for me, and her mum ordered a Chai latté!

'What's that?' I asked her.

'It's like a herb tea,' she said.

'Any caffeine in it? I asked – I don't do caffeine!

'No,' she said, 'all natural.'

I tried it and I liked it!

After breakfast we said our goodbyes and as she was hugging her daughter I heard her mum say, 'Remember what we said?'

The journey to Holyhead started off very quiet, but I figured she was just needing time with her own thoughts and was probably thinking about leaving her family – after all this was an emotional time, plus it was a considerable distance between them.

About thirty minutes into the journey I enquired, 'Are you OK? Second thoughts?'

I looked over and she had tears streaming down her face.

'Oh, oh?' I thought, 'Is the answer to that question, Yes?'

I pulled in to the next lay-by we came to. I stopped, switched off the engine, then I let the silence envelope us, before eventually saying, 'Listen? If you don't feel this is right for you, just tell me.'

But she put her hand up to my mouth and said, 'Just hold me, please?'

I naturally did this and then gently asked her, 'What's wrong?'

She took a deep breath, then told me how both her parents last night said some really hurtful things about not only her, but me, and it had really upset her.

I said I would be really surprised if they hadn't said something? 'If you were my daughter, I might be doing more than just saying words that might offend.'

'I can't believe you're defending them,' she said. 'They told me I'm stupid and that I am still a child?'

'You are!' I countered, 'in their eyes. They are trying to get you to understand, because they love you. So they need you to hear at this stage. They're just wanting you to think! I love you and I am just saying you don't want to be carrying bitterness in your heart towards them – so, for a second put yourself in their shoes and look at it from their perspective?'

She looked at me and said, 'Stop being so nice! At this very minute I hate them for what they said and the things they also called you?'

After ten minutes I sensed she was thawing a bit so I smiled and said, 'Fuck them, ha-ha – but it could be worse …'

'How?' she said.

'Imagine if they were RIGHT!

At that we both laughed.

We carried on with the journey. When we got onto the boat three and a half hours later we were almost back to normal in temperament. We decided to go to the onboard cinema, where we joined the equivalent of the mile high club, but on the sea! Mood was excellent once again. I always have enjoyed the boat – a far more civilised way to travel as opposed to bloody flying!

# Chapter 13 – Hello New Life

By the time we got to Bangor the time was getting on but, thankfully, my sister had gotten the keys and turned on the heat for us. We jumped in the shower and headed to bed pretty much straightaway when we got home! The next day was Thursday and we had no real plans. I wanted to show her a bit of the town we were going to call home for the foreseeable.

Bangor is a seaside town – which was one of the reasons I'd picked it. We both liked beach walks and just sitting looking at the waves. We went for a walk and I told her a bit about this North Down town – about how I used to work close to here in my youth. We had lunch al fresco. It was a nice relaxing day.

'I am starting work on Monday, so let's just chill out for a couple days,' I suggested.

I had arranged with Lee to hire a van to go over to England and collect everything from Kian's – which he was happy to do the following weekend!

Because it would be another week before we got our bed, we weren't really getting a brilliant night's sleep. But, hey ho, another thing I had noticed about my love

– which I believe I have mentioned before – is that she is not really a morning person and unless you wake her in a certain way she can be grumpy. But I had developed a skill set which usually put a spring in her step and satisfied me at the same time!

Lee collected all our furniture and delivered it to us as requested on the Saturday – but, unfortunately, he couldn't bring the scooter – just not enough room. Oh dear!

The house was starting to come together nicely and life was slowly but surely becoming almost normal. I was enjoying the work and was surprised at how I didn't seem to be hankering after a self-employed status again. I just didn't feel the need for all the hassle that came with it. She was also working part time, so we were getting on with living.

A friend of mine invited us to his wedding and I commented it might give us a chance to suss out this hotel. 'It's in a nice spot and could be a possible venue for us?'

'Are you serious?

I said, 'Of course! We have been together over three years, now, so it's time to make it official – and considering we never really had an engagement party, it will be a great excuse for us to have one!'

I had unleashed Bridezilla – aagh! Every opportunity she got to talk about weddings – whether it be venue, food, numbers, photographers – aagh! She did make me laugh, but it was her big day and I was just the willing participant.

We went to my mate's wedding, but she didn't like the venue, so we went to two or three places to look at and we found a place that she loved. We spoke with the Function Manager and agreed date and menu. I arranged to bring a deposit within the week and we went home happy.

I was intending to go back to the hotel on Friday evening on the way home from work, but on Thursday night while she was out at work my phone rang and it was a withheld number?

'Hello?'

'Please don't say who this is.'

'OK,' I said, 'but I am here on my own at the minute, anyway?'

'I need to ask you something, but first *please* give me your word you won't say what we talk about?'

I was intrigued. 'OK,' I said.

'What I am about to ask you is hard. I'm not really asking – I'm begging you. I need a favour?'

'I'm listening?'

'Firstly, please give me your word you won't mention this call – on your oath?'

I pondered my response for a second or two, not knowing what was coming, but eventually I said, 'You have my word.'

'Thank you. I am trusting you're a man of your word, so I have to accept it!'

'Oh, I'm delighted to hear it!' I said, sarcastically.

There was a long pause: 'Hello, you still there?'

'Yes. Listen, you say you love her, right?'

'Yes, and I do!'

'If you do then please do this?'

'Do what?' I asked.

'Send her home – to Wales. Say you need a break, or something, and make it sound like you want to finish it!'

'Are you crazy?' I said, laughing. 'I'm not going to lie and hurt her! Are you serious?'

'Listen. If you are so sure of both your feelings then let her go to get her back – and if in about six or eight weeks you can come over, if you are both of the same mindset, then you will have the family's total blessing! I know what I'm asking is hard, but her place right now should be at home, at a time when the family need her. We only ask you leave her alone for a period of time! You say you love her?'

They started listing reasons I should do the 'decent thing' and finished with, 'Prove it!'

I was totally gobsmacked, 'Listen, I am happy to let her go home any time she wants, to see her family? She is her own woman, not my prisoner you know?'

'She won't accept that. She is soul-tied to you, but if you set her free, then she will have free will. And if in a month or two you turn up and she accepts you, then no one will interfere ever again. I know it's a big ask, but you say you're secure in your feelings? So?'

Then silence.

'Soul-tied' is an expression I've heard before, when people in the church are praying for soul-ties to be broken in a person's life – like addictions and the like!

'I don't know,' I said. 'I'm not deliberately going to hurt the woman I love at the behest of YOU! I really need to think about this.'

'Well, remember you gave your ...'

I didn't need to hear the rest of it – I just hung up the phone!

As someone who believes in the power of prayer I started to pray hard. I had to pick her up from work at ten pm – an hour's time. My stress levels were way up. I can honestly say I have over the years had battles going on in my mind over a number of things, but the kind of war going on in my head at that very minute was like never before.

We had heard her Mum and Dad were going through a rough time, but when I had suggested her going home for a couple of days, she wasn't up for it at all. You know, it's at times like this that if I had something on my mind and needed to talk to someone it was always her I could talk with. She was my best friend, confidante, and in truth, I think we had had about three arguments since we got together! 'Once again,' I thought to myself, 'when my life is going well – BANG! something throws a grenade into the middle of it!'

I really steeled myself to think totally unselfishly. 'Am I too old? Are we soul-tied? What about kids? When I am ready to retire she will still be in her prime?'

In truth the more I took myself out of the equation, the more the voice on the phone made sense – plus, in my heart of hearts I thought maybe this was what needed to happen for <u>us</u>!

But could I survive without her?

She interrupted my thoughts by calling me to see where I was, as she was finished work?

'Sorry, I didn't notice the time. Give me five minutes.'

I went to collect her and, thank goodness, she was tired and headed for the shower, then went straight to bed with a headache. Part of me was relieved, because I thought she could read me and know something was up.

Now, over the years I have had some sleepless nights, but none as bad as the night I had just had. I got up at six o'clock, jumped into the shower and headed to work early, leaving her sleeping.

If I was being judged on my work ethic that day I would have come up short. I just wasn't in the mood, but thankfully, others covered for me, as I had done for them before. I was dreading going home. I couldn't face it, I just couldn't handle the situation. As luck would have it, by the time I got home she had already gone to her job. She'd left me a note, saying she had been called in early and would bell me when she finished. She signed off with, 'I love You.'

My heart couldn't handle it!

I decided to give Roger a call and I told him part of the story, saying, 'I'm thinking of sending her home.'

'After all the crap you went through to be together?'

To say he was shocked was an understatement, but he went on to say that it had to happen at some stage, because of our ages! I listened to what he had to say – after all, he'd had young girlfriends himself and he was an authority on the subject – he thought! I knew he believed he was helping me, but really, I was glad of the distraction. It helped me switch my brain off for a while. I finished the conversation by asking him if he would pick her up at Holyhead if I sent her on the boat?

'Of course,' he said.

One thing I knew was I could depend on Roger no matter what decision I made.

I was off the next day and Sunday so I knew I needed to sort this sooner, rather than later. She phoned me at eight pm to tell me she was finishing early. Could I come collect her?

'Be there in five, lovely,' I said.

First thing she asked when she got into the car was, 'Did you pay the deposit to the hotel?'

I had honestly forgotten all about it, 'No,' I lied, 'Curtis and Nicola called, so I never got a chance.'

'Aw,' she said, 'did you have a nice time with them?'

I nodded and she started telling me about her day. We got into the house and I offered her a glass of wine, which she took.

'I might just jump in the shower,' she said, 'while you're doing dinner, OK?'

'I thought we would do carry out tonight?'

'Great,' she said, 'Chinese?'

'OK,' I said.

'I will have my usual,' she said, as she headed upstairs to take a shower. I ordered the food, then I started praying for the words I was going to use to do this!

The food arrived almost at the same time as she came down the stairs. Damn, she had never looked better! We ate and talked about nothing in particular. I filled her glass, then we sat on the sofa. All of a sudden she looked at me and said, 'What's wrong?'

I took a deep breath – here goes!

I said, 'I think you should go back to Wales.'

'For how long?' she said.

My heart was pounding and my head was going to explode. 'I have got you a one way ticket,' I said.

I could see her mind working as it dawned on her what I was saying.

'What? Why? Two days ago we were booking our wedding? What has happened? I thought we were happy?'

It was killing me to watch someone I loved, whom I cherished, hurt so much. I started to hug her, but her sobbing nearly broke me. Then she tensed up and snapped at me, 'It's your family, isn't it?'

'What are you talking about? I asked.

'Well, you tell me your kids visit and then you tell me you're dumping me – what would you think?'

I was very tempted to let her think that, but I couldn't do that to my children. I tried to explain that that was not case at all, but now her temper was rising and she went on the attack, 'Right you want rid of me? Fine!'

She ran up the stairs to start packing. I heard her crying. My heart was breaking, but I was past the point of no return!

About thirty five minutes later she came rushing down the stairs and was heading for the front door.

'Wait,' I said, 'where are you going at half twelve at night?'

'Well, you don't want me here, so I'm going,' she said.

'Enough,' I snap, 'sit down.' The look of rejection in her eyes put another knife in my heart. To be honest I would have loved to get the person who'd called me and slap them hard!

I took her to the sofa where we sat down. I just held her, let her cry. She sobbed as she looked at me. She said, 'Don't you love me anymore?'

I held her hands and tried to get her to believe, 'It's because I love you that I'm doing this.'

'Well, I will never forgive you for doing it!'

I just held her for the longest time and she drifted in and out of sleep. Every so often her sobs and tears affected me and I was filling up myself. I really wanted to wake her and tell her the truth. I wanted to scream and shout about the fucker who was making me do this – but I also knew that for the first time in my life I was putting someone else before me!

At about 6.30 am I gently woke her and explained that she was booked on the ten o'clock boat to Holyhead. I had arranged for Roger to meet her and give her a lift home.

She looked at me with such hate and shouted, 'You have it all sorted don't you? You selfish bastard, you've had your fun and now you just cast me aside. Well, with any luck I might meet someone nearer my age, who can grow with me – not like you, you old fucker! Everybody tried to warn me that this would happen.'

I knew she didn't mean it, so I let her vent.

'You will <u>never</u> find anyone to love you as I did,' she said.

'Past tense already,' I thought!

I lifted her case, along with her bag. As she got into the car she started crying again. This time I said nothing. We drove without talking.

As we got close to the drop off point at the docks she said, 'There is something not right about this? There's something you're not telling me? What am I missing? Are you sick?'

'No,' I said.

'One day I will find out the truth!' she said.

'Please tell me the truth,' she said. 'Why are you doing this? I won't be angry, just tell me the truth?'

'Just believe me,' I said, 'In time you will realise I was right to do this!'

As we stopped I got out and took her case. I went to embrace her – she quickly snapped away and all I saw was anger, or was it hate? I knew she was hurting! She walked away and didn't look back. I followed her with my eyes till I knew she was on the boat. Then, and only then, did I let my guard down.

I climbed into my car and cried like a baby. I was hurting, but I gathered my thoughts as I had to call Roger to let him know what time her boat would arrive! I didn't really want to chat, and thank goodness he understood, so I hung up and started heading home – crying the whole journey. The only thing I had left were thoughts, regrets and memories!

# The End?

# About the author

Graham has been a chef since the age of fourteen. He has a passion for catering and hospitality and is recognised as someone who is respected in the industry.

His interests outside of the kitchen are in writing recipe books and being involved in local radio, where he presents his own twice weekly show.

Graham was married for 25 years and has a family of four. Two of his recipe books are now available – see below.

Big G's
AFTERNOON
DELIGHTS
A COLLECTION
OF SIMPLE, FUN
RECIPES FOR
CAKES AND
BISCUITS.
by Graham McClements

Available from your local *Amazon* store …

… with more to come!